THE CRUCIFIED JESUS

The
CRUCIFIED
JESUS

by

Fr Manasseh Youhanna

ST SHENOUDA'S MONASTERY
SYDNEY, AUSTRALIA
2012

ST SHENOUDA MONASTERY
8419 Putty Rd,
Putty, NSW, 2330
Sydney, Australia

www.stshenoudamonastery.org.au

ISBN 13: 978-0-9805171-8-7

Cover Design:
Hani Ghaly,
Begoury Graphics
begourygraphics@gmail.com

CONTENTS

ABOUT THE AUTHOR

EARLY DAYS AND EDUCATION:

Father Manasseh was born in August 1899 to pious Christian parents in the village of Hoor, near the city of Mallawi. His parents had both come from clerical families with outstanding Christian backgrounds. During his boyhood, his father passed away, and his mother took care of him under the loving eyes of his venerable grandfather. Because his mother was pious, full of wisdom, generous in spirit, generous to the poor, and merciful to the widows and orphans, and to those who were suffering, he appreciated her qualities and tried to emulate

7

them. In addition, he was very intelligent, a clear thinker, and had a keen mind.

He loved his church, and from the time he was about twelve years old he took an active part in it, and listened carefully to the sermons, taking their messages to heart. His zealous feelings for Christianity moved him to dedicate his life to the service of his church where he was ordained a deacon. He joined the Theological School in Cairo at the age of sixteen, in 1915. The head of the college, Youssef (Bek) Mankarios, hesitated to accept him because of his young age, fearing that the course of study would be too difficult for him.

After he had been in the school for a few months, the dean and the professors admired greatly his brilliance. He continued at the top of the class throughout his studies and was an excellent example to his colleagues, in character, wisdom and deep thinking. He found that his studies in the classroom were insufficient to satisfy his desire to learn. Therefore, he read all the books he could find about the Coptic Church, as well as books written by great theologians and historians. He studied all these books with great care. After five years, he graduated from the School of Theology.

PREACHER:

In the last year of his study, he was called to preach in the Cathedral of Saint Mark in Cairo. The people listened carefully to him and admired his method of preaching, even though he was young.

When he graduated from the theological school, he was appointed a preacher in the Coptic Church of Mallawi. The people in this church were unaccustomed to hear a 20-year-old man. After a few months, they found him a very deep thinker, a pious preacher and a great teacher as well as an honest leader. Thus, all the people loved him deeply.

When the people of Mallawi read in the newspapers that the Bishop of El-Minya decided to move Fr Manasseh from his church to the church at Samalut, they became exceedingly upset and rejected the move. They chose representatives to meet with the Bishop and advise him of their feelings. The Bishop quieted their fears and promised that he would not move him. He stated that the reason for the proposed move was that when he preached at the Samalut church, at the invitation of the people, they liked him and his preaching and requested that he be appointed to serve their church. However, the Bishop did not grant their request for he knew that the people of Mallawi wanted him to stay with them.

Because of his noted preaching abilities, two other Coptic bishops independently tried to interest Fr Manasseh in leaving Mallawi and coming to their churches with the promise of a much higher salary. He did not accept these offers, preferring to remain in Mallawi because of the sincerity and love of the people, ignoring the promise of a high salary.

During that time, he wrote a huge volume on the history of the Coptic Church that was published for the first time in the Press of el-Yaqzah in Cairo in 1924.

PRIEST:

On 25 January 1925, Fr Manasseh was ordained a priest in the Coptic Orthodox Church of Mallawi on the total recommendation of the people of the church. The day of his ordination was one of celebration among the various denominations in Mallawi, all of them congratulating each other.

The life of Father Manasseh was a continuous struggle with many responsibilities in the service of his church and his pastoral calls, teaching and preaching. In addition, he also was involved in reading, writing and publishing. In the last nine years of his life, he published 15 volumes, among them The History of the Coptic Church. He also published many spiritual and literary articles in newspapers and bulletins and served as editor and publisher of the Bulletin 'Paradise.'

During the national movements in 1919, Father Manasseh spoke frequently in favor of unity and brotherhood and of struggle for the progress of the nation. He was an eloquent speaker.

Father Manasseh convinced the people of Mallawi to celebrate funerals for three days only rather than their custom of celebrating for one or two weeks. He also held conferences for his colleagues, the priests and preachers of neighboring towns, to improve the service within their churches.

During his short life, he sustained various trials, enduring them with patience. None of his sons lived beyond infancy. He also suffered ill health. On December 2, 1928, his mother, whom he loved greatly, passed away. This caused him considerable sorrow. However, none of this stopped him from continuing his services to the Church until he became bed-ridden.

On Friday, May 16, 1930, he mentioned to his visitors that he was going to die that night and he asked that they would pray over his body in Mallawi and that he would be buried in Hoor. The morning of May 17, 1930, the people learned that he had passed away, as he had foretold. They went to his house with heavy hearts, awaiting the funeral. When they saw the coffin they were moved to tears, and the Moslems requested to carry the coffin, saying to the Christians, "Let us do our duty toward him because he was faithful to us during his life as he was faithful to you, and he served us as he served you. Our sadness is not less than yours." The funeral procession continued until it reached the Coptic Orthodox Church where they prayed over his body. A number of speakers eulogized him praising his virtues. The coffin was then taken from the church in Mallawi to the town of Hoor.

Finally, Father Manasseh Youhanna who had served the priesthood for five years, struggling hard like the early Fathers of the Coptic Church, was laid to rest in the hands of God.

AUTHOR AND HISTORIAN:

Even though he lived for only 31 years, he was the author of the following published books, all in Arabic:

The Way to Heaven; The Crucified Jesus; The Sun of Righteousness; The Shining Light: A Guide to the Holy Book; The Vial of Precious Perfume; The Complete Evidence for the True Faith by St. Athanasius the Apostolic; The Solution of the Problems of the Holy Bible; The Life of Adam; History of the Coptic Church; Saint John Chrysostom or the Preacher of the Two Cities; The Correct Evidence on the Influence of Christianity; History of the Spread of Christianity; Father

Manasseh Youhanna's Rebuttal to the Criticism of Father Lewis Shikhu of his Book on Church History.

Father Manasseh was a well-known religious author whose writings were theologically sound with deep meditation. His command of the modern Arabic language, which he used in his books and articles, was very strong and well organized. His writings attracted the older generation as well as the young. His book, The History of the Coptic Church, covered the history of this church from the time of the coming of Christ to Egypt in the First Century up to the Twentieth Century, followed by the history of the Popes of Alexandria through all the periods, encompassing about 2,000 years. The book also includes the relation of the different governments with the Coptic Church through the centuries, the most famed martyrs, the heresies, the establishment of monasticism, the monastic Fathers and the most important people of the Church, the persecutions, the Arab conquest of Egypt, Islamic rule in Egypt, relation between the Moslem rulers and the Coptic Church, and the relationship between the Catholic and the Protestant missions and the Coptic Church. The History of the Coptic Church is considered one of the best books written on the subject by an Egyptian in modern times. It gives an excellent and detailed representation of the struggle of the Coptic people and their church against the Romans, the Byzantine emperors, and the Moslem rulers up to modern times.

PREFACE

Our holy and heavenly Father who, for the great love You have for us, sent Your Son to be crucified. I come to You with a broken and a contrite heart, asking that Your Holy Spirit guide these words so that they maybe be as good seed falling on fertile ground. I ask that Your Holy Spirit may use the merits of the cross to prepare hearts for faith in You and reliance on the worthiness of Your Son through His death for the sake of eternal salvation.

O Holy Spirit of God, Light of the Church, let Your light shine upon the pages of this book so that we may see the cross in all its beauty and that all who seek salvation may ascend to heaven through it.

O blessed Son of God, proclaim Your cross to all, so that

they may discern it and look to it, trusting that You desire their salvation.

To You, O Holy Trinity, be the honour and worship now and forever. Amen.

INTRODUCTION

In the wilderness, when Moses the prophet observed the thorn bush unharmed by the flames of fire, he said, "I will now turn aside and see this great sight, why the bush does not burn" (Ex 3: 3) and God called to him out of the midst of the bush, and said, "Do not draw near this place. Take your sandals off your feet, for the place where you stand is holy ground" (Ex 3: 5).

As you draw near this awesome sight of The Crucified Jesus, stand in reverence and sever all your worldly attachments. Prepare for the outpouring of grace that will come upon you from the Cross.

The Crucified Jesus is the essence of Christianity. Without it, is like life without God, the body without spirit, the bride without groom, the river without water, or day without sun or light.

So gaze, toward the Cross as toward the spring of your salvation, the source of your deliverance, the root of your happiness in this present life and the assurance of attainment of eternal glory in the coming age.

CHAPTER 1

Garden of Tears

"My soul is exceedingly sorrowful, even to death" (Matt 26:38)

During their time of sadness, the exiled Jews would hang their harps upon the willows by the rivers of Babylon. They would sit beneath the willows mourning Zion (Ps 137). In this way, Christ also chose the Garden of Gethsemane on the Mount of Olives for His own mourning and grief (Matt 26:37). He chose the olive, for its bitterness, as an indicator of His suffering, and because the dove brought the good news of deliverance to Noah using an olive leaf. Humanity received the good tidings of salvation from death in this very garden.

In this garden, to which David escaped from his son Absalom (2 Sam 15:23-30) and onto which the righteous king Josiah dispersed the dust of the idolatrous altars (2 Kings 23:12), sorrow and distress seized our Master so that He openly declared it to His disciples saying, "My soul is exceedingly sorrowful, even to death," (Mk 14:34).

These are words that undoubtedly elicit tears from the eyes of all who love Him. They affected His disciples to the extent that they longed even to sacrifice their own lives to save their Master from what would befall Him. He cried out to all people that they might bear what grieved the soul of the Saviour. He cried out to them that they might partake of His suffering. His disciples, however, had not even the strength to keep vigil with Him for one hour.

Let us then enter the Garden to contemplate this spectacle where our eyes will gaze upon a sight to wound the heart and melt the emotions. There we will see the New Adam in the Garden struggling, not for His own gratification but for the salvation of mankind.

There is a great difference between these two gardens: the

first brimming with the means of joy and rest, the second infused with the signs of sadness and grief; a fertile garden and a barren one; a garden in which the creature found rest and one in which the Creator found none; a garden where began mankind's misery and the other from where springs of happiness for the sons of Adam emanate; one where we fell and the other where we were raised; a garden where Adam was condemned and the other where his debt was paid by Jesus.

"How marvellous is the wisdom of the indiscernible God: the blameless One is punished for the offence of the sinner; the righteous One is scourged for the crime of the wicked; the upright One bears the guilt of the hypocrite; the Master pays the debt of the bondservant; the Creator recovers what has been discarded by the creature," St Augustine

The soul can be afflicted with two kinds of distress: one is that of physical pain, and the other of mental anguish; and on that night, the Lord Jesus suffered from both, anticipating the severest of pain to His body and suffering the full gamut of mental torment.

Here then is a sight to ponder: He said to his disciples "Stay here and watch with Me," and then went a little farther, fell on His face, and prayed, saying, "O My Father, if it is possible, let this cup pass from Me; nevertheless, not as I will, but as You will," (Matt 26:38,39).

What a marvellous demonstration of extreme humility and what a sublime example of the truest prayer. He, through His obedience, healed the wounds of disobedience and A touching scene to affect the hardened, but unaffected itself by time: The Son of God, coessential with His Father, fallen to the ground!

He who is in the bosom of the Father grieves that His soul is exceedingly sorrowful. He, whom all the heavenly powers worship, falls and kneels!

Who can be a witness to this poignant scene and not be moved? Whose heart is not devastated at seeing the Almighty One humbling Himself and the exalted One stooping? What exceedingly abundant love this is that has caused the Son of God to surrender Himself to such shame!

In anguish, He turned to prayer to His Father in order to teach us that prayer is the weapon of the struggling believer Who hears the requests of others and accepts their pleadings. Christ prayed fervently, and you, O believer, when you are in the midst of your tribulation, have courage and pray. He prayed in order to sustain those who pray. He "prayed that if it were possible, the hour might pass from Him," (Mk 14: 35).

Yet how could this be? He came to die, so how is He now seeking to escape death? He came for the cross so how does He now desire to evade it. He prayed in this way to set a good example as to how we should act in the midst of our tribulations. He did not, therefore seek to retreat but to teach us an important lesson for He said, "No one takes it from Me, but I lay it down of Myself, I have power to lay it down, and I have power to take it again," (Jn 10:18).

Jesus did not anticipate the cross only on that evening, nor did He perceive it only on the day of His crucifixion but rather from the first day of His earthly life and even from the beginning of time. It was always before Him as alluded to in the Psalm, "And my sorrow is continually before me," (Ps 38:17). He therefore not only foresaw the cross prepared for His torment, but also knew of all that would befall Him in the way of humiliation, insults and torture. Every prisoner, no matter his offense, has some hope of being saved from his imprisonment, but Jesus never expected to evade the cross. On His way with His disciples to Jerusalem, Jesus "began to tell them the things that would happen to Him," (Mk 10:32). "Behold, we are going to Jerusalem, and the Son of Man will be betrayed to the chief priest and to the scribes; and they will condemn Him to death," (Matt 20:18).

Many people react adversely when they experience a sudden calamity. How much greater was Christ's grief and sorrow, reflected in the words of the Psalmist "For my life is spent with grief, and my years with sighing," (Ps 31:10), knowing all along that the cross awaited Him. For this reason Jesus repeatedly mentioned the cross in His sermons saying, "he who does not take his cross and follow after Me is not worthy of Me," (Matt 10:38) and "If anyone desires to come after Me, let him deny himself, and take up his cross, and follow Me," (Matt 16: 24) and His words to the sons of Zebedee, "Are you able to drink the cup that I am about to drink," (Matt 20:22). These and other verses show that not one hour passed, in Christ's earthly life, when He did not carry the cross for the sake of the salvation of mankind.

Jesus, then, in His entreaty to His Father, did not fear an unforseen event, for He had anticipated every step to the cross and had passed through each with majestic fortitude, knowing it to be inevitable. This is the joy of the cross - Jesus did not deviate from it but was steadfast in His purpose. He was not a victim of chance but rather fulfilled all prophecy in every step He took, making it a matter necessitated by the will of God, "Behold, we are going up to Jerusalem, and all things that are written by the prophets concerning the Son of Man will be accomplished.

For He will be delivered to the Gentiles and will be mocked and insulted and spit upon. They will scourge Him and kill Him. And the third day He will rise again," (Lk 18:31-33). When they came to arrest Him, the Bible says, "Jesus therefore, knowing all things that would come upon Him, went forward and said to them, 'Whom you are seeking?'" (Jn 18:4).

At the end of the Saviour's first struggle in prayer at Gethsemane, He returned to find His disciples asleep. How lamentable! Your disciples have abandoned You and You have been left to bear Your grief alone. Your fallen creation that You have come to renew, has slept leaving You to wrestle alone for its deliverance. Earlier You had foretold of Your suffering and had addressed them saying, "My soul is exceedingly sorrowful, even to death," (Matt 26:38), and had asked them to keep vigil with You for company and consolation in Your anguish. Instead, You found them neglecting the obligation of a friend in the time of need, and You rebuked them as one rebuking his beloved saying, "What! Could you not watch with Me one hour?" (Matt 26:40). They added to Your sorrows for they embodied the creation which did not value the matter of its own salvation, and so has neglected the One who accomplishes it.

The Saviour advised them saying, "Watch and pray, lest you enter into temptation," (Mk 14:38). Even in the midst of His distress, He did not neglect to bestow goodness on others. How great is Your compassion, dear Jesus, and how sublime is Your desire for the salvation of mankind. Let us heed the Saviour's advice on the night of His agony - pray, lest you enter into temptation. Keeping vigil allows us to pray, and prayer keeps us watchful.

Let us thank God when trials intensify, for they will not come unless one is able to face them with prayer, prevail and rejoice in the victory. So many overlook their own salvation and fling themselves upon the bed of negligence. God cautions them in various ways and they are still heedless. Whereas Jesus is concerned with the salvation of man, man is found to be indifferent. How great is Your compassion, dear Jesus, for You are long-suffering and I am neglectful and insensible. Awaken me, O Lord, and do not allow me to be overcome by the sleep of the vanities of this world.

The Saviour got up once more anticipating the overwhelming pain and sorrow that would confront Him. He left His disciples asleep and alone rose as a mighty champion to endure the arrows of agony. He repeated His entreaty but submitted His will to God that we may learn how it is necessary to submit to Him in our own trials.

He said to His Father, "O My Father, if this cup cannot pass away from Me unless I drink it, Your will be done," (Matt: 26:43). Truly, the greatest knowledge is the knowledge of the will of God, the greatest valour is submission to it and the greatest vocation is its accomplishment.

"And when He returned, He found them asleep again, for their eyes were heavy; and they did not know what to answer Him," (Mk 14:40).

"So He left them, went away again, and prayed the third time, saying the same words," (Matt: 26:44).

The heavenly hosts were troubled when they saw Him praying as a servant. The mighty One humbled Himself for our sake and the exalted One stoops to our level. His prayer was effective for an angel from heaven appeared to Him to strengthen Him (Lk 22:43). Here we find great consolation for all who pray following the example of the Saviour. Help from the Lord will certainly come to reveal to him that "those who are with us are more than those who are with them," (2 King 6:16). Let the praying faithful be reassured then, because of God's promise, "Because He has set His love on Me, therefore I will deliver Him," (Ps 91:14). So take courage and enter the Garden and there you will find the angel who will strengthen you: the angel of peace in the house of sorrow; the angel of fortitude in the house of distress; the angel of the resurrection in the house of death.

The Savour prayed with such fervour, "His sweat became like great drops of blood falling down upon the ground," (Lk 22:44). St Jacob of Serug said:

"To an ill man, sweat is a good sign as it heralds recovery of health. The sweat of the Son of God fell as He worked to rescue His handiwork from the depth of the abyss. Adam was afflicted with the great sickness of death - Jesus came and perspired that Adam may have rest from his affliction. Through the Lord's sweat, health was restored to the ailing servant. In the sweat of his face Adam ate his bread (Gen 3:19), but this sweat which was mingled with sin was not able to bring healing, and so He, who is without sin came and sweat once for all, and saved him from his sins."

In the Garden, Christ was sweating at the mere anticipation of His suffering - how much greater must have been His agony when this suffering became a reality. Who is not affected by this situation, and who is not pained by his own sin knowing that it was that which caused the Son of God to sweat in the anguish of anticipation. Know this, you sinner, that what caused the sweat of Your Saviour to flow was not the torment He awaited but your many transgressions! Lord Jesus, in order to purchase medicine for my ailing soul You paid a truly exorbitant price. So let all the earth exalt You and let every breath praise Your great name.

Behold love wringing the pure body of the Saviour to yield abundant sweat! Consider, O man, the extent of your wretchedness that when your God wished to weep for you, He shed tears not only from His eyes but from every pore in His body in such abundance that they appeared as great drops of blood, as proof of His great love for you. What manner of thanks is due to You, O Son of God, for this struggle and this sweat! The blood of the martyrs and that of the rest of mankind, from the beginning of time to its end, is nothing compared to a single drop you shed in the garden.

In the Garden, before the Saviour's body was hung on a physical cross, His soul was hung on a cruel spiritual one. As He contemplated what was about to happen to Him His soul suffered the greatest of pain. This was compounded when He saw the traits of treason and extreme feebleness in His creation as well as that of denial of His great goodness. As all this depravity appeared before Him and so He was grieved knowing that He would die for the sake of those guilty of it so that each drop of His precious blood became as if a second hell to the obstinate callous sinner.

The prophets had formerly foretold the emotional anguish, "My heart is severely pained within me, And the terrors of death have fallen upon me," (Ps 55:4) and "The pains of death surrounded me, and the pangs of Sheol laid hold of me; I found trouble and sorrow," (Ps 116:3). In this Christ resembled Isaac of old, for when He was in the Garden of Olives, He prepared Himself for sacrifice upon the cross as Abraham prepared the wood and placed it on Isaac's back to offer him up as a burnt offering to the Lord. In that very hour He could see all the means prepared for His torture and could hear the cruel cry of "Crucify Him!" belonging to those who had disregarded His goodness toward them. He could also see the conspiracy that Judas plotted with the Jews for His destruction. He looked down upon Hades to see the devil and his host stirring up the chief priests and the people, and looked up to heaven to see the Father accepting of His sacrifice, for He Himself had accepted the salvation of humanity.

The primary cause, however, of His sorrow in the Garden was that He became sin for us, as it is written in the prophecy, "All we like sheep have gone astray; we have turned, every one, to his own way; And the Lord has laid on Him the iniquity of us all," (Isaiah 51:6). Let us imagine that Jesus, at that moment, saw the sins of the past and of the future, those of all humanity, the offenses of young and old, crimes committed and wrongs inherited, and these all gathering together as dark clouds into one point and descending upon His blessed person like a mighty and fearsome tempest.

His heart was like a deep brimming lake into which flowed thousands of streams signifying our sins and transgressions – a debt He had accepted to discharge, though He Himself was spotless. "Because He had done no violence, nor was any deceit in His mouth," (Isaiah 53:9). Truly "He made Him who knew no sin to be sin for us, that we might become the righteousness of God in him," (2Cor 5:21). God's testimony of Christ is that He is holy and innocent of all sin which is in agreement with Christ's own words to the Jews, "Which of you convicts Me of sin? And if I tell the truth, why do you not believe Me?" (John 8:46) and "the ruler of this world is coming, and he has nothing in Me," (John 14:30), and with the words of the apostle, "For we do not have a High Priest who cannot sympathize with our weaknesses, but was in all points tempted as we are, yet without sin," (Heb 4:15) and "For such a High Priest was fitting for us, who is holy, harmless, undefiled, separate from sinners, and has become higher than the heavens," (Heb 7:26) and "how much more shall the blood of Christ, who through the eternal Spirit offered Himself without spot to God," (Heb 9:14).

Christ's sinlessness is then a prerequisite to His atonement for our sins. The mystery of redemption is that God, Who knows no sin, became sin for us. The burden of all humanity was laid on Christ as a load would be laid on the back of a man, and on His head as the high priest of old had placed his hand on the head of the sin offering for the atonement of himself and of his beloved people (Lev 16:6).

So why was it necessary for Jesus to endure all this sorrow, distress and torment with which He was afflicted and the severe agony that He bore in patience which tore at His bowels and set His heart ablaze? Indeed in order for Him to bear our sorrows and to purge our pain, He surrendered Himself to extreme sorrow obediently and willingly, even eagerly and compassionately, that He may transfer us from eternal sorrow and everlasting pain to an endless life of joy.

Our Saviour was saddened and groaned due to the unparalleled immensity of the sins of the world that was placed upon Him.

When Ezra lamented the sins of the people of Israel, he described it as weighty and great. How much heavier were the sins of the whole world that were borne by the Son of God Who, according to St John, is the One "who takes away the sin of the world!" (Jn 1:29). If even one person's sins are unbearable, as

Cain declared, "My punishment is greater than I can bear!" (Gen 4:13) and as King David pronounced, "For my iniquities have gone over my head; Like a heavy burden they are too heavy for me," (Ps 38:4), how much more so were those of all of humanity, "who Himself bore our sins in His own body," (I Pet 2:24). As the Apostle John wrote, "He Himself is the propitiation for our sins, and not for ours only but also for the whole world," (I Jn 2:2).

For if the smallest sin committed is an eternal offense against God's glory, and this offense deserves an eternal punishment, how much more so the multitude of sins of the entire world? How then can the advocate Jesus, who is vigilant in guarding His Father's glory, leave these innumerable hideous sins without redress? He judged it a necessity to be inflicted with countless and varied afflictions for the sake of countless and varied sins. When He took it upon Himself to repay our debts, He became responsible before His Father for all sin and accountable for its recompense.

The prophet Nathan said to David, "The Lord also has put away your sin," (2 Sam 12:13). Be glad and rejoice, then, o sinners for the sin of the all humanity has been lifted from you to be placed upon the shoulders of Christ.

Contemplate, O my soul, your sins that have saddened your Master - your blasphemy, your infidelity, your indulgence in your pleasures and injustices and especially your disobedience, all manifested in your denial of His suffering for your sake. They are what caused the sweat of the Son of God to form like drops of blood. When an only child dies, his parents lose all comfort. So how much greater was Christ's sorrow, for the sake of the multitude of souls that perish in eternal destruction.

Truly, the Son's acceptance of death on behalf of all sinners is the greatest triumph. The Garden of Gethsemane was the setting for the greatest battle witnessed by history, not withstanding its personal nature. In this battle, we witness a struggle between two paths - light and darkness. Christ had to decide whether to retreat from the cross, giving the powers of darkness victory, or to accomplish man's salvation no matter the cost to Himself. Consequently, when the Saviour uttered the words, "Father let it be according to Your will not Mine," He opened the door of life to all. From that moment, He set out toward His goal in serenity coupled with majesty. He rose above the anguish and left it behind for all eternity. The darkness in the Garden was nothing but the shadow of His Father's wings. The Patriarch Jacob had formerly entered this fearful darkness - he had wrestled with the Angel and had come out of the struggle with a new name and a new nature. In this way, the Son of God had come out victorious in the Garden since He had accepted death for the salvation of the world. Yes, Jesus accepted to drink the cup full of wrath, in order to bestow upon us the cup of salvation that quenches.

Come then, O my soul, and hasten to the Garden of Gethsemane, and contemplate your God who had said, "My soul is exceedingly sorrowful, even to death," (Matt 26:38) and say to Him, "Why do You suffer and why do You weep? Are You, Who encouraged many of the martyrs to endure, afraid? Indeed the martyrs received courage from You and You took upon Yourself our fear. You deserve all the goodness and we all the evil. Fear then is mine, and the power Yours: Your dishonour belongs to me, and my glory and honour are Yours for all time."

Be attentive and know that while Jesus was in the Garden, He was occupied with the payment of our debt. The cause of His sorrow was sin. Beware, then, lest you are found to be one of those who grieved Him and caused Him this great anguish. For, if you are found to be blameworthy, how then will you be able to lift your eyes to your Saviour and not wither with shame as you observe Him sorrowing for you? If you are so hard-hearted that your Master's sorrow does not distress you, then at least grieve for your sins that are the cause. Take care to remember His kindness and not to cause Him to shed even one more tear.

CHAPTER 2

Jesus Arrested and Judged

"Then the detachment of troops and the captain and the officers of the Jews
arrested Jesus and bound Him" (Jn 18:12)

Now, my Lord Jesus Christ, the time has come for You to be rewarded for all Your sweat and for all You have endured for man's salvation. St Jacob of Serug said:

"Threats, rage, humiliating uproar, derision and gnashing of teeth over the pure blood. The hay hastened to create a quarrel with the flame! The dirt and dust confronted the gale that can uproot mountains! The clouds and billows went out to threaten the blaze! The shadow became deranged and attempted to restrain the sun! He asked them 'Whom are you seeking?' and they drew back and fell to the ground for the dust has no power to challenge the tempest!" As Isaiah the prophet foretold, "He was oppressed and He was afflicted, Yet He opened not His mouth;" (Isa 53:7). Perhaps this prophecy was on the mind of John the Baptist when he witnessed for Jesus saying, "Behold! The Lamb of God who takes away the sin of the world," (Jn 1:29). When our powerful Saviour gave Himself up to His adversaries, it was by His own desire and consent. His arrest was not due to helplessness, nor His silence to unawareness, but rather He yielded Himself up willingly. Many times silence is actually a sign of reliance on God and forgiveness of adversaries, besides being a Christian duty indicating spiritual strength and self-control. The actions and conduct of a person speak louder than his words.

Why were You silent, Jesus? The slightest insult provokes us to take revenge, but You were silent. You are the Almighty who, with one word, could crush them. When they sought You, You responded with calmness and authority, "I am He," and they drew back and fell to the ground (Jn 18:4-9). Why then, O Lord, did You surrender Yourself to their cruel and severe punishment. Why did You not petition Your Father to provide You with more than twelve legions of angels? (Matt 26:53).

Jesus answers saying, "For this purpose I was born and for this I came into the world." Indeed, You endured all this and were long-suffering for Your love of the salvation of mankind.

Then the troops and officers from the chief priests came and arrested Him and tied Him up. They pounced upon Him like rabid dogs and fierce lions and bound Him so violently that the ropes began to strip the skin off His hands. He had said of Himself, "The Spirit of the Lord is upon Me, Because He has anointed Me To preach the gospel to the poor; He has sent Me to heal the broken-hearted, To proclaim liberty to the captives," (Lk 4:18). For this reason He allowed them to bind Him, so that He may take the place of man who is bound by sin and tied up with the fetters of iniquity.

What hand was this that dared to bind the benevolent hands of our Saviour? O the callousness of my heart! Wretched man that I am, for it was I, my God, who bound Your holy hands! How many times have You desired to stretch out Your grace-bearing hand to me which I tied and pushed back with my indifference, negligence and ingratitude? Grant O Lord, from this time forward, the grace to obey Your holy guidance and never to oppose Your blessed will. Stretch out Your hand and do to me as You will, for I am Your obedient child.

They bound the Saviour and dragged Him through the streets of the city to the chief priests to be scorned, disgraced, insulted and abused. Some slapped Him brutally and others struck Him on His back. They pulled Him so aggressively that He fell to the ground and then they kicked Him to induce Him to rise. How the multitude must have crowded around Jesus to see Him in this state and to rejoice in His humiliation!

Who is this who is being dragged through the streets as like a lowly beast and is being trampled like a helpless worm? It is He, at whose name "every knee should bow, of those in heaven, and of those on earth, and of those under the earth," (Phil 2:10). It is a wondrous thing that the angels did not hasten to rescue their Lord from the hands of the unjust. How is it that zeal for the glory of their creator did not move them to take revenge upon those who humiliated Him? But this was His will, and so the angels concealed their weapons in obedience to Him who was being despised by humanity.

After this they led Jesus to Annas the father-in-law of Caiaphas (Jn 18:13). There He was surrounded by the wicked. "He who opens and no one shuts, and shuts and no one opens," (Rev: 3:7), was imprisoned in the house of Annas. Annas then sent Him onto Caiaphas who asked Him about His doctrine. Jesus answered him, "'Ask those who have heard Me what I said to them. Indeed they know what I said.' And when He had said these things, one of the officers who stood by struck Jesus with the palm of his hand, saying, "Do You answer the high priest like that?" Jesus answered him, "If I have spoken evil, bear witness of the evil; but if well, why do you strike Me?"' (Jn 18:19-23).

How cruel a hand and how savage a heart! How, O wretch, did you dare to raise your hand to this regal face before which the angels tremble? How did you have the audacity to strike the God who has prepared, for you, all this goodness upon the face of the earth, and who has breathed into your nostrils the breath of life? Tremble O heaven, groan O earth and be darkened O sun over this scandalous insolence, and judge between your Creator and His creation, for he who abused Him was not the greatest of judges but rather the lowliest of servants.

The servant came forward and struck the Son of God on His cheek. The heavens were troubled for He did not command it to strike this man with thunderbolts of indignation, and the earth was astonished that He did not ask it to open up and swallow him. Nevertheless, the Son of God consented to be inferior to a servant in order to set at liberty those who are oppressed (Lk 4:18).

With even greater astonishment, we now witness what the creature offers its Creator. They slapped the face upon which flowed abundant tears because of their destruction. They struck the head that had borne the burden of their sins. They spat upon His face that the prophecy may be fulfilled, "I gave My back to those who struck Me, And My cheeks to those who plucked out the beard; I did not hide My face from shame and spitting," Is 50:6.

How great is your faithlessness, O man, and your denial of your Creator's benevolence? Rather than for the utterance of words of gratitude and for the proclamation of His marvellous works, you have used your tongues to heap abuse upon Him and your mouths to hurl insults and spittle upon His pure face!

God created us to honour Him, but we have offended Him - the Lord of honour was insulted! The God of glory was humiliated! But you, O sinner, if you desire to console the Son, wash the filth of your soul away with words of repentance. With this act, you will have washed away the spittle from the face of Christ, for you were made in His image (Gen 1:26).

They took the Lord to Pilate who began to question Him. St Jacob of Serug said, "The clay wielded the sceptre of judgement over his Creator. The Judge of all judges Himself was judged by the deluded, but remained silent. The Truth was humbled and falsehood exalted. Sin was elevated and the righteous One slapped. The wounded condemned the Physician who sought to heal them." Why, in this manner, was the Light wronged, the Righteous tortured, and Justice abuse? The Lord answers saying, "My law, that is My abundant and eternal love for your salvation, is the ultimate judgement. I have loved you with an everlasting love and so I have granted you mercy."

When Pilate knew that Jesus was from Galilee, he sent Him to Herod. "That very day Pilate and Herod became friends with each other, for previously they had been at enmity with each other," Lk 23:12. Truly, wherever Jesus is, there also will be peace and reconciliation. He defused the anger of both the governor and the king, reconciling them to each other as a precursor to the reconciliation between God and fallen man that He would effect "having made peace through the blood of His cross," (Col 1:20). "Then Herod, with his men of war, treated Him with contempt and mocked Him, arrayed Him in a gorgeous robe, and sent Him back to Pilate," (Lk 23:10-11).

Through all this, Christ remained serene and majestic. Pilate retried Him but was astonished at His calmness and tranquillity. Many are embittered by injustice and grumble, but He endured injustice quietly. Pilate wished to show Jesus to the Jews in this critical state, having seen His battered and severely beaten body, crowned with thorns and bearing a reed rather than a sceptre. He led Him to a platform and cried out before all saying, "Behold the Man!" (Jn 19:5). All who would have seen Him in this condition would join Isaiah the prophet in saying, "He has no form or comeliness; and when we see Him, There is no beauty that we should desire Him," (Is 53:2), and He would then rightly proclaim, "But I am a worm, and no man; A reproach of men, and despised by the people," (Ps 22:6). His state could not affect these cruel people, nor His afflictions soften their hearts and they cried out demanding that He be crucified.

Pilate did not wish to carry the responsibility, for he could discern Christ's innocence, and so he washed his hands saying, "I am innocent of the blood of this just Person. You see to it," (Mat 27:24). Nevertheless, he recanted and ordered Christ to be crucified. How many people, after having washed themselves in the waters of repentance, return again to crucify the Son of God through their backsliding and sinfulness? (Heb 6:4-6)

O my blessed Saviour, where are you now? In the courthouse! Were You not the One who stood in their synagogues teaching their ignorant, and in their houses and streets healing their sick. Why are You now being judged? Who are these brutes who have arrested You? Weep and wail you daughters of Jerusalem, not with mere tears, but from the depths of your hearts, for they have bound and shackled your Bridegroom. Let us all weep for Jesus Who was bound for the sake of all sinners. Our sins and transgression, and His desire for our redemption, are the reason for His fetters.

The devil was given permission to use all his power and authority to bring about the torment of Christ. He roused the mob to use all means of torture, as Christ Himself reveals, "this is your hour, and the power of darkness," (Lk 22:53). This was also the case when he formerly attacked Job with many afflictions, though he was not permitted to take his life. Who would have thought that the Source of the life and the Physician of wounds, of all humanity would allow Himself to be subjected to this extent of satanic abuse and distress, which He endured in a desire for our salvation?

How glorious You are Jesus, for you preferred pain over comfort, adversity over rest, dishonour over Glory and the cross over Your throne carried by the Cherubim! You gave up Your privileges so as to restore to us the goodness we had lost and You were impoverished in order to enrich us. O my Master, to You is the glory and the honour.

As for you, O my soul, follow your God along the way from Gethsemane to Golgotha, to see how much abuse He endured for your sake. Consider His honour and eminence and that He is the incarnate Word of God, possessing absolute goodness and true glory. Consider by whom He was rejected - Judas who hunged himself and Pilate who died in despair. Accept Him happily for He is your Beloved, and there is no other beloved like Him.

Look down upon me, O my God. The world seeks to chain me with its love, the devil to bind me with his deceptions and the flesh to tie me down with its lusts. I no longer crave salvation, because of all these shackles, unless Your grace liberates me. I ask You, my Lord, to give me true freedom from slavery, as You promised, "if the Son makes you free, you shall be free indeed," (Jn 8:31,36).

Truly, my God You were willing to yield to the evil one in order to free me from his captivity. You consented to be tied with ropes to free me from the bondage of my sins. You accepted the disgrace that is rightly mine, due to my transgressions, and so I thank You from depths of my heart and so does the multitude of Your angels and all Your saints.

CHAPTER 3

Jesus is Scourged

"By whose stripes you were healed" (1 Pet 2:24)

The Saviour was condemned to death by crucifixion, and they scourged Him according to Roman custom. This practice was particularly brutal because they used to strip the condemned, tie them to an arched post and whip them across the back. The Roman whip was made from pleated bulls hide, knotted on the ends and within each knot was inserted a piece of bone. Whenever the whip struck the bare back of the condemned, it would leave a very deep and painful wound.

It was common for those that are scourged to become unconscious or to die from the unbearable pain. Those assigned this task were Romans soldiers who had no compassion for any Jew, as they despised the entire Jewish nation and afflicted them with harm whenever they could. They would sometimes goad each other on to do as much injury as possible even to the extent of spilling the bowels of the condemned.

Let us contemplate the Almighty God Who adorns every living creature, naked, tied to a pole and the soldiers taking turns to scourge His holy back, with whips, chains and spiky ropes, until He was were bruised, His flesh torn and His blood flowing, thus fulfilling the prophesy of Isaiah the prophet, "From the sole of the foot even to the head, There is no soundness in it, But wounds and bruises and putrefying sores; They have not been closed or bound up, Or soothed with ointment," (Is 1:6).

How could these callous and unfeeling soldiers not be moved to compassion by the awesome and incomparable beauty of the Son of God? Indeed, the loveliness of flowers and the beauty of the scenery cannot hold the clouds back from pouring rain and hail furiously upon the fields and gardens. Similarly, the divine beauty of Jesus could not affect these cruel-hearted people to refrain from torturing and abusing Him.

What evil did He ever commit against you, that you should torture Him in this way without mercy or compassion? What harm, offense or injustice has befallen you from this immaculate body that you should wound Him so violently and not grieve for or lament Him? You have shed His precious blood though He gave it to you as life-giving drink. You have torn His holy body with your whips and beatings though He offered it to you as sustenance. Woe to you sinners! Have compassion upon Him who shows you compassion and pities you in your afflictions, and grant Him rest in His pain and suffering. What more would you do to Him who has become wound upon wound?

Do You, the meek Lamb Jesus, endure all this suffering for a fallen and contemptible creation? How is it that You neglected and abandoned Yourself to this extent in order to love a despicable and offensive little worm? You endured for it unparalleled pain, pain that far exceeds all the sins of the earth and the waters of the depths of the sea.

A single drop of blood issuing forth from these wounds is of infinite worth and value. Truly, Your love for us is boundless. You were merciful to others but not to Yourself. The Jews were amazed by this and said, "He saved others; Himself He cannot save," (Mk 15:31). You saved Isaac from slaughter, rescued the three youths from the fiery furnace and snatched Daniel from the mouths of the lions. Why then do You permit Yourself, to suffer so cruelly? You are renowned for Your mercy toward others, why then Jesus, were You not merciful to Yourself?

It is written concerning the righteous man, "No evil shall befall you, Nor shall any plague come near your dwelling," (Ps 91:10). How then do I see You now, the Holy and Righteous One, covered in wounds and bruises?

"Listen o man," says the Lord, "the love with which I have loved you is what compels Me to be so severe upon Myself. I came in the likeness of sinful flesh (Rom 8:2) in order to save you from sin, and to rescue you from its snares."

Oh my Master, You consented, in the abundance of Your love, to be wounded and scourged for our transgressions, and so You said through your prophet, "For all day long I have been plagued," (Ps 73:14).

We give thanks to You O blessed Son of God, for all You have sacrificed. And you, O sin, how devious and deceitful you are - you have caused my God to suffer all this agony. Let the world end speedily, so you, and those who committed you, may descend to hell.

They whipped our Saviour so severely, that when Pilate witnessed the scourging and the wounds inflicted, he thought that this would placate the Jews. The Romans themselves loathed this form of torture and limited its use to the lesser elements of Roman society. When it was discovered, for example, that St Paul was a Roman citizen after he had been beaten with rods, the magistrates were struck with fear. Even the barbarians only scourged thieves and murderers. How then did the Son of God, endure this shame, though He is Lord of heaven and earth and the Wisdom and Might of God?

The Angels must have been astonished at this spectacle and bewildered at the amazing condescension of the Son of God. At His birth, they had sung a hymn of peace. What a predicament to find now that He is covered in excruciating wounds.

Come, my soul, and hover over the palace of Pilate, and witness your Saviour stripped of His clothing and left alone in the midst of an assembly of wicked men, with no defender or advocate. He did not protest or complain nor did He utter a word in His own defence. How could this disgraceful scene not move hearts?

O my soul, if this world tries to attract you to its futile pleasures and vainglories, take refuge in the wounds of your faithful Saviour to find rest and peace, as a dove finds rest in its abode. Truly, nothing banishes the love of the world, and convinces us of the vanity of all it has to offer, like the wounds of our good Saviour. These are the wounds that, once perceived by St Thomas, caused him to utter the cry, "My Lord and My God," (Jn 20:28).

St Augustine said, "If Thomas wanted to approach the wounds of Christ in order to be healed of his doubts, we also ought to draw near to receive healing for our ailments and cure for our intentions," We need to come near to be healed of a death that is borne everyday by our deceitful intentions and warped resolution. Hasten, you wounded, to the Healer of wounds. Come, all you who are wounded by the arrows of sin, to Him who accepted these arrows in His own blessed body.

Contemplate well, O my soul, the sight of your God, in the hands of those cruel soldiers, faint with His blood spilt on the ground and having bruises all over His body. Remember that Jesus suffered all this for your sake. "But He was wounded for our transgressions, He was bruised for our iniquities; The chastisement for our peace was upon Him, And by His stripes we are healed," (Is: 53:5).

Contemplate O my soul, you who cannot bear a cruel word spoken against you, how Christ bore our grief and carried our sorrows (Is 53:4). Contemplate how He bore insults, by a wicked people, patiently and calmly for your sake. So if your God bore your illnesses and your infirmities, how is it that you cannot bear those of your neighbour? Moreover, if He accepted the chastisement due you, to cure your sicknesses, why do you not collaborate with Him in this matter of your cure? Instead, I see you adding to His wounds with your perverse deeds. Why do you not hate the sin that has injured your Beloved Jesus? Why do you cling to it as you would to a beloved, and disregard the offering of your Saviour as you would that of an enemy? Let sin be abhorrent to you. Grind and scatter it as Moses did with the moulded calf, and trample it, keeping your gaze continually upon Him they abused for your sake.

How great is Your kindness, rich Your mercy and generous Your goodness, O Jesus. How great is my negligence and serious my shortcomings, in giving thanks for Your great and holy majesty. Grant me O Lord, the grace to have Your wounds perpetually before me so that I may not forget You. Teach me to endure all things with thanksgiving, as You did, so I may be worthy to be truly Yours.

CHAPTER 4

A Crown of Thorns is Placed on His Head

"When they had twisted a crown of thorns, they put it on His head"

(Matt 27:29)

Before sin entered into the world, the Earth never yielded thorns. Thorns grew as a result of sin. After the fall, God said to Adam, "...cursed is the ground for your sake; ...both thorns and thistles it shall bring forth for you," (Gen 3:17-18).

The earth was devoid of harm or injury before the fall, but after sin it became replete with danger and hazard. The adverse effects of sin are twofold: it harms both body and soul. As the earth yielded thorns to prick the body, so sin and its punishment have become two thorns to torture the soul and conscience of man. St Paul said, "For the wages of sin is death," (Rom 6:23).

The first thorn is sin and the second is death - the punishment for sin. Sin became for man a sharp, painful and fearsome thorn from which there was no escape. Even the many sacrifices that were offered could not reassure or comfort him but rather the cry of every man became, "O wretched man that I am! Who will deliver me from this body of death?" (Rom 7:24).

The second thorn, death, described by the Apostle Paul as the "last enemy", has stung and troubled all. Jesus consented that all these thorns, that had been for the torture of humanity, be gathered together for Him to be crowned with. He "condemned sin in the flesh," (Rom 8:3) and we therefore rejoice saying, "For the law of the Spirit of life in Christ Jesus has made me free from the law of sin and death," (Rom 8:2). So by the incarnation and death of the Saviour, the thorn of sin has ceased to exist. St Paul said, "And if Christ is in you, the body is dead because of sin, but the Spirit is life because of righteousness," (Rom 8:10).

Through the death of the Son of God, death no longer has power over the believer, and the Christian will sing in victory, even on his deathbed, saying, "O Death, where is your sting? O Hades, where is your victory? The sting of death is sin, and the strength of sin is the law. But thanks be to God, who gives us the victory through our Lord Jesus Christ," (1 Cor 15:55-57).

A certain Christian said, "Whenever I looked at a grave and saw the dead being buried and covered in earth, I fell into despair. Now all has changed and the fear of death has vanished. I can now say as I depart to heaven, 'O death where is your sting?'" Hear now the answer from the cross "It is on the head of the Son of God", for He has pulled out the thorn of death from me and embedded it into His own head. Death no longer holds any dread. There is no doubt that if you remove the sting of a scorpion, you would not fear it more than you would an earthworm. Similarly, the sting of death has been removed and it therefore no longer holds any sway over us.

What is astonishing is that the creation, for whom the Son of God came to abolish the stings of sin and death, is the same that crowned Him with thorns. As St Jacob of Serug said, "He came to remove the thorns from the earth. He bore the curse of the earth through the crown they placed on His head, and the burdens of the whole world as a mighty One. The sins, offenses, sorrows, pain and injury were twisted along with the crown and placed upon His head for Him to carry. He abolished Adam's curse with His crown of thorns and eradicated the curse of the land that had killed generations while it lasted. By His crown of thorns, He has crushed the dominion of Satan who sought to be a god over creation."

Come let us contemplate this momentous incident. When the soldiers tired of beating Him, they twisted a crown of thorns, and gave it to the most savage of them all. He took it and pushed it violently into the head of Jesus so that the thorns pierced His temple wounding it. Yet Jesus did not complain in the least. The extreme pain, though, produced considerable tears to fall to His cheeks, and mingled with the blood flowing from His wounded head. His blood mixed with His tears – a healing balm for all nations.

Consider, O my soul how those cruel soldiers drove those thorns into the holy crown and temple of Jesus, and how each of these thorns penetrated deep down to the brain. If you can picture this happening then acknowledge the greatness of the pain emanating from it. Could you bear such excruciating pain? Can you even imagine it? How remarkable then was the fortitude of Jesus, His precious blood flowing over His face and neck, His eyes gazing, lifeless and His heart full of sorrow and anguish.

Reveal to me O most precious Head, how immense Your pain was when the thorns pierced You. If a single thorn can make a young person or a woman cry in agony, or send a wild beast of prey howling and darting through forest or dessert, how can we perceive the enormity of the pain You endured my Lord? You in whom they thrust thorns – not in Your hands or Your feet but in Your most noble and sensitive crown, and in Your gentle brow, even Your holy head, in a deadly way.

Who has ever heard, seen or read that a crown of thorns is used in place of a regal crown? Pilate had not commanded it and neither the Romans nor the Jews had ever used it. These wicked men had contrived it in order to transform the glorious Kingdom of Christ to a kingdom of mockery and shame. Out of envy they twisted this crown to add to His immense suffering. Let us be assured that this evil did not benefit them at all, but rather brought upon them more shame and degradation and made us heirs to a healing salve to save us from Satan's oppression.

Indeed the forests of Palestine were not void of other crowns that were more appropriate for this great King. But evil man was not capable of offering his Creator anything but evil. God rejoices in goodness and in the one who offers it up to Him, but how can the evil offer up goodness?

O my faithful Saviour, King David had said of You, "And You have crowned Him with glory and honour," (Ps 8:5). How then can I look at You now crowned with a crown of thorns, You who crowned man with every goodness and blessing? How then can he repay You, for Your endowment, with this cruel crown?

O you sinners, mingle your tears with this blood flowing from the head of your Saviour. Bow down in reverence to this head crowned with thorns. It is the head that is raised above all heads and exalted above all that is lofty.

Imagine O sinner, a beautiful flower in the midst of thorns or a delicious piece of fruit surrounded by thistles. This was your lovely Saviour who is "fairer than the sons of men," (Ps 45:2). He was crowned with thorns. He was, as was said of Him by His beloved, "Like an apple tree among the trees of the woods, So is my beloved among the sons," (Song 2:3). How then can you see the thorn wounding the heart of your King and not be saddened? How can you permit your Lord and Master to be tortured and not attend to Him at least with your tears? Enough are the insults you brought upon your Lord through your sins and enough is that each of your sins was as a sharp thorn piercing His blessed brow and His pure heart. From this day, come let us offer the thorn of contrition that we may know the extent of pain caused by that cruel crown.

O My Lord Jesus Christ, who is this who has treated You so

unjustly? Who is this who has been so cruel? Who has caused Your holy head this unbearable pain? Indeed, I have caused all this through the multitude of my sins and offenses. It was I who pierced Your holy crown with these sharp thorns by my defiled thoughts, and by daring to raise my own head in pride and arrogance. It was I who caused Your eyes to weep by focusing my own onto earthly vainglories. I caused You to sorrow through my attachment to the pleasures of this vain world. Oh my Saviour how cruel I am? My sins are the thorns that pierce and cut into Your holy head. How many times have I mocked You, as the Jews have done, with my false promises and vain pledges? How many times have I vowed myself to You and then broken the vow? Help me O my God and let Your grace be my companion, that I may be sanctified by Your Holy Spirit and may begin a new life bearing the fruits of faith, hope and love.

CHAPTER 5

Jesus Carries the Cross

"And He, bearing His cross, went out to a place called the Place of a Skull, which is called in Hebrew, Golgotha" (Jn 19:17)

Pilate presented Jesus to the Jews in this most wretched condition, after he had Him scourged, crowned with thorns and frightfully abused, in the hope that they may have pity and release Him. It was as if he was saying to them, "See in how many ways I have insulted and abused Him so that perhaps your hearts may soften toward Him," but that only heightened their cruelty and they cried out the more, "Crucify Him. Crucify Him!" (Jn19:6). There Jesus stands, O man, so have compassion on Him, you who have scourged Him with the straps of your sins, crowned Him with the thorns of your haughtiness and wounded Him with your offenses. How then, can you withhold your compassion while He suffers for your sake? Remember that He is the Son of your beloved God, who would not be afflicted but for your sins. Observe to what extent your transgressions have taken Him. O that you may reflect on this and hence deepen your sorrow, discarding your callousness.

When the crowds would not desist from their cries, Pilate handed the Lord over to them to crucify. He condemned to death the Spring of Life. He delivered the holy and righteous One into the hands of the wicked. How great is your iniquity, O Pilate, for you delivered the blameless One to protect your position and rank. Nevertheless, how many times have I, the wretched one, done the very same thing? How many times have I offended Jesus in order to honour men? How often have I conformed to and feared their opinions whilst defying and violating His commandments?

After the sentence of death was pronounced, they led the Saviour away to the place of crucifixion. The custom was that the condemned person would carry his own cross. The Lord carried this heavy load until He collapsed under it due to the effects of torture and lack of sleep. The soldiers flogged Him to force

Him to carry His burden once more only to see Him fall to the ground again. How grieved we are for You Jesus, the full God who upholds all things by the word of His power (Heb 1:3). How is it that You collapsed under this piece of wood while in You all things consist (Col 1:17) and by Your will they exist and were created (Rev 4:11).

Let us attend as Jesus replies, "It is not under the burden of the cross that I gave way but under the weight of all those sins placed upon me, for they are heavier than steel and lead. And yet I have borne all this heaviness as something trivial or even desirable, for My love for you lightens the load of your sins on my shoulders."

It seemed to the world that at that moment, that Christ only carried the cross. In reality, He carried all of the sins of humanity. The body carried the cross while the soul carried the sins. His body bore the fatigue of our bodies while His soul carried the afflictions of our souls. He willed to be our substitute, carrying the burdens of our bodies and souls in His own body and soul.

O You the meek Lamb, You were wearied from the journey when You sought a solitary soul and found rest by Jacob's well (Jn 4:6). But now, as You seek all souls, why do You not stop to rest from Your immense agony and suffering? Grant me, though I could not share in Your suffering, to at least weep over and deeply regret those sins that were Your burden.

Contemplate, O you pure rays of sunlight, a sight you have not witnessed since God placed you to shine over the pages of this creation and since your cloak was thrown over the shoulders of this land. Indeed, you beheld Isaac carrying the wood, over which he was to be offered early in the morning as a burnt offering, over isolated routes away from strangers who would see and ridicule him. Jesus, however, carried His wood in the middle of the day, in the centre of Jerusalem, trumpets before Him, drums beside Him and a crowd of people following Him. Isaac was compelled by a compassionate father, while Jesus was driven by a people who had no pity in their hearts. Isaac carried the wood for a short distance while being lamented by his father, but Jesus carried His cross a long distance while being insulted, kicked and slapped by the multitude. Isaac did not meet with his mother Sarah on his way up that hill, but Christ encountered His mother Mary on the way to Golgotha, adding to His suffering. Isaac did not carry his bundle while exhausted from lack of sleep, or wounded from head to toe as happened to Christ. Isaac was not aware of what was about to befall him, but Jesus, our Deliverer and our Saviour, knew all and fulfilled all.

Come then all you people for whom Christ endured all this. Come let us see on what seat love has seated Him and on what bed He has lain to rest from His many afflictions. They placed the heavy cross on the shoulders of the King of all creation. What horror befell the angels of heaven? What pain should afflict our hearts as we witness God, before whom all creation trembles, in this lowly state and great humility, carrying the wood of the cross and yielding under its weight, wearied and afflicted and stumbling as He walked, falling and rising over and over again. This is a tremendous load matched only by our shame as we come to understand that our sin was the heavy burden laid upon the shoulders of Him who is blameless.

What is this road leading to death on which You walk, O my God? What is this most painful bed You have prepared for Your rest? What is this most precious blood that has drawn a path from the place where You began bearing Your cross to the place of Your crucifixion?

A group of women followed Him on the way and they bewailed and lamented Him. Some of these women were affected and saddened by what they had witnessed, driven only by natural emotions for what they perceived to be an injustice. When Jesus perceived that they lacked the needed faith, He turned to them and said, "Daughters of Jerusalem, do not weep for Me, but weep for yourselves and for your children," (Lk 23:28). Even in the midst of His agony He did not forget to guide and teach the people. By this He taught us not to allow the sorrows of this world and its tribulations, to distract us from our obligations toward ourselves and the church. Rather than allowing our emotions to be the only basis for our sorrows, we ought to reflect on the majesty of His abundant love and absolute sacrifice, so that if we weep, we do so over a denied grace and a rejected kindness, seeking pardon and acceptance through our remorse.

Grant me O my God to pity myself, for You were innocent as You carried the burden of the cross, whereas I without a cross am oppressed by the burden of my sins. St John Chrysostom said, "For what reason did Jesus will that Simon of Cyrene help Him carry the cross, though He had borne the torture and the pain alone? The Saviour wished to make us understand that without our own cross, His holy cross was not sufficient. If we seek salvation, we ought to follow Christ carrying the cross with patience and submission to His divine will, following our divine Teacher to death."

How content we would be if we discern how to follow Christ, on this journey, bearing the cross of tribulation and suffering in this world, for He said, "Take My yoke upon you and learn from

Me, for I am gentle and lowly in heart, and you will find rest for your souls. For My yoke is easy and My burden is light," (Matt 11: 29-30).

In order to walk in the footsteps of Christ we need to reject, in our tribulation, all human comfort. Only then will we feel an immeasurable and deep sense of contentment and peace. How can these tribulations possibly affect us when, in the past, the cross was shameful and fearful, but now after it was borne by Christ it is honourable and satisfying?

The Apostle Paul said, "Therefore let us go forth to Him, outside the camp, bearing His reproach," (Heb 13:13). Do we not see that Jesus died outside where there is shame, while we reap the benefits of His death and remain in repose within? Do we seek a home, a place, a name or a possession in a world where our Lord and Master was renounced and rejected? Do we crave honour and status and do we seek riches and esteem in a world where our Master found nothing but a manger, a cross and a borrowed tomb?

Be aware that a man cannot live a life in this world without a cross - that is free from trials and tribulation - and that it is futile to attempt to flee from adversity. Do not think that only the children of God experience hardship, for the adversity and misery of the wicked is far greater. Though they do not meet with abuse, their lusts will hound them and their twisted consciences will prod them. All the sons of Adam carry the burden of suffering and hardship, but those who suffer least are the believers. Their cross is fleeting, light-bearing and fruitful, for they bear it in this life only. After death, they will have rest from all their afflictions, and God will wipe away every tear from their eyes (Rev 7:17).

St Augustine said, "This short life is a tribulation", and "If you say you have not yet suffered anything, then you have not begun to be a Christian." In addition, Saint John Chrysostom said, "Tribulation is a chain which cannot be unlinked from the life of a Christian". This is because the believers live in a world in which everything is contrary to their hopes. Fire and water are quiet as long as they do not come together, but as soon as they meet, the water begins to seethe and evaporate, and this struggle continues until either element is eliminated. Righteousness is contrary to evil and the children of God are contrary to those of this world. The children of God shine and always seek that which is lofty, while the wicked are cold and consumed by the world. The Christian who seeks to become too comfortable in this life will not follow Christ bearing his cross. St Paul carried a heavy cross throughout his life with Christ, but he still remarks, "For our light affliction, which is but for a moment, is working for us a far more exceeding and eternal weight of glory," (2 Cor 4:17). He considered his burden to be light for it was transitory and would be followed by eternal glory, the memory of which gave him consolation in the time of tribulation. What then can be said of us if we avoid bearing our light cross, even for this brief time, given the words of the Saviour, "Most assuredly, I say to you that you will weep and lament, but the world will rejoice; and you will be sorrowful, but your sorrow will be turned into joy," (Jn 16:20).

The cross of the wicked, however, is long-lasting, unbearably heavy and devoid of any reward. To each of the two thieves crucified with the Saviour, belonged a cross. The wicked one wished only to be freed from his cross, but it would not leave him and followed him into hell. The thief on the right, however, endured his cross carrying it for a few short hours leaving it behind as he entered paradise. Similarly, the rich man, who lived in pleasure throughout his life, descended to his torment, while Lazarus, who bore the cross of poverty throughout his, reposed into the bosom of Abraham. The yoke of Christ grants rest while that of the devil is followed by nothing but groans, distress and eternal suffering. Many suppose the yoke of the evil one to be lighter than that of Christ but, in reality, it is heavier than any yoke because it brings its bearer to eternal torment, while the yoke of Christ brings one to absolute and everlasting repose.

We ought not then ask of God that He lift His cross from us, whenever we are engulfed by misfortune, but rather we should endure patiently being comforted by the words of St Paul, "if indeed we suffer with Him, that we may also be glorified together," (Rom 8:17). If our souls are in need of encouragement, let them run to meet the Beloved Jesus outside the palace of Pilate. Pursue Him, O my soul, bearing your cross, seek Him in the throng and when you find Him, retreat with your Beloved. Ponder His frailty and marvel at how the One, who carries the entire universe with one word, falls under the burden of the cross. He who upholds the heavens is unable to bear the cross and collapses under it as if dead, in order to teach you the value of the cross and the honour of bearing it.

O my good Lord, You have fallen under the burden of my sins, which You bore in my stead, in order to reconcile me to Your Father, and You fulfilled the words, "The plowers plowed on my back; They made their furrows long," (Ps 129:3). Which sinner, O Jesus, can see You thus and his heart is not softened or his eyes are not filled with hot tears? Who can see You carrying the cross for his sake, exhausted from the immense loss of blood and not be moved inwardly?

So weep, my wicked soul, for Jesus carries the cross for your sake and nothing will lighten His burden nor comfort Him but that He see you repenting of your sins. Knowing the torture awaiting sinners adds to His torment. Let us heed His words, "For if they do these things in the green wood, what will be done in the dry?" (Lk 23:31). For if sin has caused all these woes to Him who is blameless, what will your lot be my depraved soul, you who are ranked with a dry twig prepared for fire? If the holy Son Who said of Himself, "Though I have stolen nothing, I still must restore it," (Ps 69:4), (that is restore to Divine justice what was owed by sinners) suffered all this, what will become of you, you who have robbed the glory of God with your sinfulness and enmity?

How then can I love sin after witnessing the torture of the Beloved, Who is pure and devoid of any fault? I thank you Jesus that You have accepted all this suffering on my behalf to free me from the debt of sin. If You find me a dry twig or if You see within me a callous heart, temper me with the oil of Your grace and soften me with Your honourable blood. "Create in me a clean heart, O God, And renew a steadfast spirit within me. Do not cast me away from Your presence, And do not take Your Holy Spirit from me," (Ps 51: 10-11).

CHAPTER 6

The Crucified Jesus

"Who for the joy that was set before Him endured the cross,
despising the shame" (Heb 12:2)

On the cross we encounter two extremes: the very best and the very worst. The best emanates from God and the worst from man. In God, nothing was found but goodness while man offered nothing but selfishness and dishonour. The cross demonstrated the beauty of God and the hideousness of man, for on the cross, God extended His love while man his enmity, God His salvation and man his corruption, God His goodness and man his wickedness.

Let us lift our eyes to the cross and ask, "Who is this who has embraced the wood of the cross, and who has consented to die this disgraceful death?" Death is fearful. Who is this who has dared to give Himself up to it with such courage? He had said of Himself, "No one takes it from Me, but I lay it down of Myself. I have power to lay it down, and I have power to take it again. This command I have received from My Father," (Jn 10:18). He has then surrendered His life by His own authority and offered Himself up by His own will.

Why do You not, O crucified One, fear death as do all others and what has prompted You to offer Yourself up to it with such amazing courage?

I will proclaim to you all from My cross that which I have desired for your sakes, that when I saw death, dreaded and barring the way to your salvation, I scorned its perils and loved it for the love of you. When I saw that the cross was an obstacle in your path to success, I disdained it in order to save you. It was love that made the cross more desirable to Me than the throne of glory. I embraced it with longing, just as a bridegroom embraces his bride, for I know that in the cross is your eternal life.

Truly, there is no greater proof of the love of Jesus than

the cross. It is difficult for us to imagine the level of contempt felt for the cross in the days of Christ. Stoning was the punitive method used by the Jews, but the Romans introduced crucifixion to Palestine. In Italy, it was used for slaves, insurgents and all those to be shamed upon their death. Apart from that, the Romans used the sword to kill any condemned person. The Law of Moses cursed all who are hung on the wood of a cross (Lev 21:23), and the intent was that this curse befell the cross of Jesus. The Jewish teachers say that Abraham sits at the gates of Hades to prevent any of his children from entering, apart from those who have been cursed by the law.

The cross was the method of execution reserved for the worst of murderers and criminals. What then has given it such great worth now? Jesus the blameless was crucified upon it transforming its lowliness to supreme greatness and its vileness to great honour. Christ has redeemed the cross also from the curse so that it has become a sign of blessing. It has become a symbol of divine atonement and the victory of eternal love, even the essence of our holy faith. The cross of shame has become the cross of glory.

Previously, there was nothing as fearsome as the cross but now it is exalted by Christians so that even monarchs proudly adorn their crowns with it. It has also become delightful and loved by the warriors of Christ so that St Andrew, on beholding the cross on which he was to be crucified, exclaimed: "Hail, precious cross, that has been adorned by the precious limbs of my Lord."

Others consider its shame but we perceive its honour, they deem it weakness while we know it as strength. "For the message of the cross is foolishness to those who are perishing, but to us who are being saved it is the power of God," (I Cor 1:18). How can we not glorify the cross when it has become a throne for the King of glory? How can we not extol it when our noble redeemer had flung Himself upon it? How can we not elevate it, while from it the Sun of Righteousness Jesus has shone forth with healing in His wings (Mal 4:2)? How can it not become the object of our pride when it has become for us a glorious ladder through which we have been promoted to the highest heaven? What is more glorious than the cross and more splendid than the transcendence of the One who glorified it by His embrace? What is more sublime than the suffering endured by the Lord Christ upon it, the sighs He raised and the precious blood that dripped from Him like sanguine pearls to wash sin away from the heart and to cleanse the world of wickedness?

The suffering endured by Christ upon the cross was both physical and emotional.   Let us meditate upon this suffering learning from the example of Christ's reaction to it:

I. His Physical Suffering

Let us observe in detail what these cruel people did and watch as they strip the Saviour of His garments, to raise Him naked upon the cross.

What is greater than the love of God, more beautiful than His patience and broader than His forbearance? How You were patient, my Heavenly Father, with these insolent people as they assaulted and stripped You of Your clothes, and how You bore those insults. How astonishing! Our great God, who donned the heavens with a robe of light and adorned the earth with a garment of flowers, has been elevated onto the cross without a single garment to cover His body.

As one of the fathers reflected, "Let us ponder how that garment, bonded to His wounded and bleeding flesh, was removed, for this would have aggravated and reopened the wounds and intensified His pain. To strip Him of the garment, they would also have had to remove the crown of thorns from His head and then to reinstate it hence aggravating and deepening those wounds as well."

Another of the fathers said, "Come let us cover Him with the garment of love, as did Shem and Japheth their father Noah, and shed abundant tears that our eyes may be blinded to the sight of Jesus naked on the cross. For even the sun veiled its light lest it glimpse the nakedness of its Lord."

Let us also witness the crucifiers, as they throw the Son of God to the ground, asking this meek Lamb to lie down and stretch out His body onto the cross that they may mark out holes for the nails. This marking was executed carelessly, and so when it was time to nail Him to the cross His limbs were stretched in a brutal and savage way.

One of the soldiers took the right hand of the Saviour and extended it to its limit, while another handed him the nail and hammer. He hammered the nail driving it right through the flesh to the wood of the cross. Then he took His left hand and when it did not reach the intended hole, they tied a rope to it to pull it out savagely causing His shoulders to dislocate. They repeated the process with His pure feet while He lay there like a lamb in the hands of ferocious beasts of prey. He felt intense pain at the realization that He was immobile, unable even to wipe the blood streaming down His face. O most cruel soldier, you who hammers the nail, how is your heart not torn as you wound the blessed hand of the Beloved, and your bowls not in turmoil as you see His precious blood flowing freely from it?

Indeed, they pierced two pure hands and the blood drips onto the ground. Two hands that had never before been stretched out except for the healing of the sick, the cleansing of lepers, the restoration of sight, the feeding of the hungry and the raising of the dead. Yes, they nailed the hands that had blessed children, hands that had only moved to bestow blessings but are now stretched out upon the cross to bestow an eternal blessing. As another of the fathers said, "Since Adam fell when he stretched out his hand to the tree of Paradise in an act of self-serving love, the New Adam was compelled to stretch out His hand in an act of selfless love, to once more restore contentment to the world."

Then they brought ropes and other lifting apparatus and began to elevate the cross, and the body nailed to it, in a way unbearably painful to the Crucified One. When they erect it in the intended position, His bones come out of their joints and all His muscles are torn as prophesied, "all My bones are out of joint," (Ps 22:14). This was all done in such an aggressive way that His hand were torn due to the heaviness of the weight borne by them. The only obvious sign of the unbearable and excruciating pain He was feeling was the accumulation of drops of sweat on His blessed brow.

It is apparent that the intent of Christ being condemned to death by crucifixion was not only His death but also the infliction of unspeakable suffering, for when they came to crucify Him they did not remove the crown of thorns from His forehead. Let us consider the effects of all this torture. First, the parts of His body penetrated by the nails were extremely sensitive containing veins and nerves, all causing bitter and unbearable pain. The method of crucifixion also caused most of the blood to flow to

His head resulting in very high blood pressure and considerable pain. The weaker His body became the more acutely the pain was felt. Through all this, Jesus was as serene as a man Who does not fear death but rather as one Who is content to face what would befall Him.

The place of the crucifixion was called Golgotha, a Hebrew word meaning the place of the skull. According to Origen, "This was because the body of our father Adam was buried there and so the Only-begotten Son came to the abode of our ancestor in order to restore to him eternal life". St Cyril also said, "The name skull is a symbol for Christ who is the head of the church". It was said that this was also the site where criminals were executed and where their skulls were discarded. The Saviour desired to restore eternal life to this place of death.

This place was outside of the city (Matt 27:31). St Paul explains in his epistle to the Hebrews; "For the bodies of those animals, whose blood is brought into the sanctuary by the high priest for sin, are burned outside the camp. Therefore Jesus also, that He might sanctify the people with His own blood, suffered outside the gate," (Heb 13:11-12). By this he indicates that, he who lingers outside the boundaries of his church and is not united with his only Lord is perpetually crucified. The mount of Golgotha is the one alluded to in the Song of Solomon, "Until the day breaks and the shadows flee away, I will go my way to the mountain of myrrh and to the hill of frankincense," (Song 4:6). This was prophecy of what the Saviour of the world would taste of bitterness, and of the sweet aroma He would lift to the Father atop this mount.

The prophet calls to us "Come and let us go up to the mountain of the lord." So, let us hasten all you sinners, to the place of atonement. Come, you saints, to see the spring of your righteousness. Come, all you women to the source of holiness and purity. Ascend it, all you Christian people, to glimpse the pulpit from which the loftiest sermon was delivered, and the most precious blood was shed to wash away your sins.

The mount of Golgotha is the house of the God, the door to heaven, the ladder of Jacob that connects heaven to earth and the paradise of delight holding both the cross and the Tree of Life. It is the mountain upon which Abraham offered his son Isaac. It is as if God is saying, "My son Adam, listen to what My faithful servant and friend had done upon this mount, he has freely offered up his only son to prove his love for Me. In like manner, I will declare My love for this broken world and offer My Only-Begotten Son as a sacrifice for your sins."

Come, you who thirst to drink water from the Spring of salvation for He is the symbolic rock from which sprang fountains of living water. Hasten to Him you wounded for He is the cluster of grapes carried from the Promised Land the wine of which heals your wounds. Draw near, o you faithful, for He is the vessel of oil from which the widow repaid all her debts. He will sustain you all, for His precious sustenance will never diminish no matter how many people approach Him.

Truly, He was battered and yet He heals who are battered. He was wounded and yet He binds the wounds of all. He was stripped naked and yet He covers all our faults.

Astonishing! Let us enquire about Him who hangs upon the wood of the cross. Is He not the holy and righteous Possessor of the throne of glory? Who is this Who suffers? Is He not the Lord of creation and its Master? Who is this whom they have raised between two thieves? Is He not the One whose place of rest is the Father's bosom? Who is this whom they have nailed to the cross? Is He not the Judge of the living and the dead? Who is this Who died upon the cross? Is He not the source of eternal life? Who is this Who endures such contempt and derision? Is He not the One from Whose Holy place fire blazed forth and consumed the transgressors of His law?

Why do You do this my Redeemer? What has induced You to accept all this? Is the great One abused? Is the glorified One abased? Is the lofty One humbled? How great is Your love and how remarkable is this strange scene. Has man ever witnessed the like of it? Who has ever heard that He, in Whose hands is life and death, is condemned to death, as a murderous thief? Has it ever happened that the just Judge is Himself judged by the lowliest of His subjects?

O my saviour, it was not those nails that fastened You to the cross, but Your indescribable love. You gave Samson the strength to free himself from his bonds, why did You not free Yourself from Your own?

Let the sun gaze well, the moon not shift from its place and all the forces of nature turn their attention toward Golgotha to see the Redeemer of sinners, for He is "a Man of sorrows," (Isa 53:3) as was said of Him in the prophecies. There was not, in His body, one member or organ left that was not in agony. His eyes were punched and bruised and His cheeks slapped and battered. His ears were tortured by insults, profanities and derision, His throat parched with thirst and His lips bitter. A crown of thorns penetrated His temple and head, and nails pierced His hands and feet. His arms were wrenched. Strong ropes were used to tie His joints and to drag Him along the ground with utter contempt and humiliation stripping the skin of His neck. His shoulders were sapped of strength due to the excessive weight of the cross.

His legs, back, chest and stomach were not spared the severe scourging He received from the unjust.

No other experienced the pain experienced by Jesus because, as all theologians agree, His holy body was more sensitive than that of any other human. Though the pain He endured exceeded any other, He bore it all with such patience and gentleness. Do you not see the honoured man, raised in comfort and luxury, distressed at smallest injury, while a poor peasant quietly endures and accepts the cold and fatigue that are his lot? In like manner, the perfection of our Saviour caused Him to feel His tortures more acutely, taste the bitterness more intensely, and smell the putrefaction more strongly.

It is regretful that the body of Christ was prepared in order to suffer, "the Son of Man did not come to be served, but to serve, and to give His life a ransom for many," (Matt 20:28). His body became a vessel in which was poured a sea of pain, torture and suffering, sufficient to wash away the filth of all humanity, for He had said of Himself, "Then I said, Behold, I come; In the scroll of the book it is written of me. I delight to do Your will, O my God, And Your law is within my heart," (Ps 40:7-8).

As someone had previously noted, "Listen all you people and be astonished, for if all the afflictions suffered by all humanity were gathered together they would not be equal to that endured by your Saviour." Abel was murdered, Zechariah was stoned, Isaiah was sawn, Lazarus was covered in sores but of none of them was it said that he was, "a man of sorrows,". If St Peter were to approach with his cross, St Stephen with his stones, St

Paul with his sword, St Ignatius with his lion, together with all the martyrs and all their pain and suffering and we compared them with that of the Son of God, there is no doubt that He would be the Champion in the arena of pain and sorrow. He alone is worthy to be called the Foremost of the martyrs and their supreme King and He alone has the right to call out saying, "Is it nothing to you, all you who pass by? Behold and see If there is any sorrow like my sorrow," (Lam 1:12).

2. His Emotional Suffering

The agony of the Son of God did not only affect Him outwardly but inwardly also. Inwardly, He was brimming with profound sorrow as the prophecy foretold, "I am poured out like water, And all My bones are out of joint; My heart is like wax; It has melted within Me," Ps 22:14. What else but shame has melted the heart of our Saviour and has torn Him apart, as He has declared, "Reproach has broken my heart, And I am full of heaviness; I looked for someone to take pity, but there was none; And for comforters, but I found none," (Ps 69:20). Here we hear Him saying to His Father, "You know my reproach, my shame, and my dishonour; My adversaries are all before You," (Ps 69:19). It is as if He wished His Father to be a witness to this great shame that wounded Him more than any other, for dishonour torments the honourable person above all else.

All living creatures in the universe, whether animals or plants, feel and suffer pain to differing degrees. Whatever pains a man, does not affect an animal, while an animal may suffer from something that will not upset a plant. A body may suffer but then is healed, but the suffering of the soul does not heal, as the wise Solomon said, "The spirit of a man will sustain him in sickness, but who can bear a broken spirit?" (Prov.18:14). How great the disparity between what Christ went through and what is befitting Him. The cross of shame was not a fitting situation for Christ Who from all eternity has been the subject of all majesty and honour, equal on the throne of glory. The cross was the lot of all humanity who rightly deserved it. Remarkably, however, it was the Rescuer who became a captive, the Judge accused, the Commander of the whole army abused, the holy and righteous One convicted and the Son of God considered a blasphemer. He who crowns us with His mercies was crowned with thorns, He who grants us His gifts and blessings, stripped naked and He who is the Resurrection and life, delivered to death!

Is there a greater shame than that of the Creator being tortured by the work of His hands or than to attribute numerous crimes and offences to the blameless One and to condemn Him to death according to the verdict of the chief priests? Indeed, it must have been easier for Him to endure all the physical torture than to bear the shame of the cross and the curse of the law! If we wished to comprehend this fully, we could imagine a king deposed by his subjects, betrayed and surrendered to his enemies, stripped of his royal garments and clothed in rags, crowned with a crown of thorns, handed a lowly reed in place of his sceptre, mocked, spat upon and shamefully struck upon the head.

Jesus Christ, however, bore this shame patiently, not because He deserved it, but in order to save humanity.

Oh my Lord and my God, who is not astonished to see You in this state and whose heart is not touched and pained with compassion and kindness. I worship You in truth, O my King and my God, and my spirit submits to You acknowledging in my heart that You alone are the true King, though You did not will to reveal Your glory or to exercise Your unrivalled power. Though you allowed Yourself to be insulted and humiliated by Your cruel enemies, You alone are worthy of the glory, the worship and the honour forever.

Let all the angels worship You and the heavenly host thank You on my behalf for this mercy You have shown me in bearing all this shame and dishonour for the love You have for me. O my King and my God, rule over my heart and my soul and let no other take me out of Your hand.

St John Chrysostom said, "The greatest of all kinds of torture is shame". For this reason St Paul said, "Looking unto Jesus, the author and finisher of our faith, who for the joy that was set before Him endured the cross, despising the shame, and has sat down at the right hand of the throne of God," (Heb:12:2). Whenever we desire to praise a person who has been victorious over many enemies at once, it suffices to mention the most powerful adversary. Likewise it is said of our Lord Jesus Christ when He died on the cross that He "despised shame". It was the greater grief that occupied Him all the days of His life as alluded to in the Psalms, "My dishonour is continually before me, And the shame of my face has covered me," (Ps 44:15) and "Because for Your sake I have borne reproach; Shame has covered my face," (Ps 69:7).

In the end it was said of Him, "Let him give his cheek to the one who strikes him, And be full of reproach," (Lam 3:30). He did not say that He had had His fill of injury, pain or scourging, for in the opinion of all theologians, the Saviour died still craving all this suffering though He had endured unbearable pain. They all agree, however, that He could not yearn for any more shame for the arrows of shame are sharper than those of pain as alluded to by the wise Solomon, (Prov 12:18).

Our Saviour is saying to every man, "Know that for your sake I have suffered rebuke," (Jer 15:15). Therefore meditate, oh you faithful, on the cross, look upon your Saviour and say to Him, "Why do you bow Your head upon the cross with brokenness of heart?" Hear now His reply, "It is because I was crucified though I committed no offense. I the innocent became blameworthy". Indeed, it has never happened that anyone has been judged for the goodness of his reputation or the purity of his conduct. Joseph was jailed unjustly but his garment was found in the hand of his master's wife (Gen 39:16). As for Christ, what was the allegation, accusation or offense levelled against Him? Not long before that, the multitude had proclaimed Him a heavenly prophet and a preacher of the truth greeting Him with the cry, "Blessed is He who comes in the name of the Lord!' The King of Israel!" (Jn 12:13). How then did He deserve to be lifted upon the cross as an outlaw?

What shame is greater than that of the Innocent who carried upon His shoulders the offences of the entire human race? Let us suppose that a rich princess, from among those accustomed to lavish living and regal robes, was commanded to wear ragged and filthy clothes previously worn by a scab-crusted man, then, wearing this same garment, forced to attend an assembly of honourable women. How great would be her embarrassment in this situation. This is analogous to what happened to the Lord when He put on the sins of the world that are more hateful to God the Father than any putrid body. It would have been better for Christ to appear before His Father in a garment covered with spiders and serpents than for Him to be draped so with the sins of the world. Why did thorns penetrate that pure head? It is because our heads are fraught with unclean thoughts. Why did they pierce those noble hands? No doubt it is because our hands are perpetually immersed in evil deeds. So whatever wickedness our members perpetrate, affected His holy members. Our crimes were transmitted to Him, our evil gazes made him weep, our pride has bowed His head, the corruptness of our hearts has caused His to melt like a candle in fire and our pursuit of sin has fastened His feet to the cross.

Let us gaze at our crucified Saviour to understand this mystery, to contemplate the reason for this cruel death and to address Him saying, "O Son of the living God! Is this your royal opulence? Is this Your divine might? Are those Your court officials and are these blasphemers lauding Your divine majesty? Is this accursed wood the throne of Your glory and have Your regal robes been dyed with this blood? So tell us, O Son of God and Glory of the angels, has Your love for mankind taken You to the extent that You would gather to Yourself all the suffering and dishonour possible though You are without blame or guilt?"

Come all you people and marvel! Why do you not truly feel the grace of the One who died for you? "Now when Job's three friends saw him in this miserable situation, they tore their garments, poured dust on their heads and cried loudly for him. Even though, they stayed seven days and nights they did utter one word to him because of their extreme sadness," (Job: 2:11–13). So how is that you, O church of Christ, do not weep for Your Lord, when you see Him humiliated by all. Grieve O you heavens for Your Maker when you see His humility, after He was transfigured before you on the Mount of Tabor. Weep O sky, wail O moon and sigh all you heavenly bodies for the Light is nailed to the wood. And you O disciples of the Saviour, why are you not here to lament your good Teacher as He dies. Come O you believers and grieve over Him who gives you the good reward. Weep and wail O you sinners for He who grants you remission of your sins offers Himself up to death. Shed rivers of tears, all you penitent, for the head of your Saviour is bowed the bow of death. Inherit the fruits of virginity you who are chaste and you who are married mourn over the bridegroom of the church.

Where are you who were once blind and whose eyes were opened by the Saviour? Where are you O whose deafness was cured by Him so that you could hear once more and you who were once mute and whose tongues He loosened? Where are you who were brought back to life though once dead? Come all of you to weep for Him as He gives up His Spirit.

Who can contemplate the sad circumstances and not be distressed? Whose bowls are not crushed when he considers this painful scene, the sight of his compassionate Saviour and this illumined face of our beloved Jesus stained with blood, as He hangs on the cross with His head lowered?

Do not weep, for His death is not death but life. Yes, they lifted Him on the cross but He ascended upon it as the stone cut without hands (Dan 2:44, 45) to become the chief cornerstone and to rebuild the broken world. They spread out His arms, but He extended them to hold the boundless universe, to carry all creation and to reconcile it to His Father. He stretched out His hands to bestow the blessing of salvation and to restore life to those over whom death reigned. They nailed Him to the cross but with these nails He freed us from our debts and nailed sin that it may no longer have dominion over us. Adam ate from the tree and died, so the Son of God took a branch from it, made a cross with which He restored life and a divine bow with which He triumphed over the forces of evil.

Behold evil is vanquished and its host flee. Behold the lust of sin is disarmed for it has become hateful, and the world overcome for it has become detestable. They all run away saying, "We thought that the cross would end His life, but instead it has exalted it. We had hoped that death would defeat Him allowing us to subjugate all mankind. Instead He has overcome us through His cross and has triumphed over us through His death and has snatched from our hands those we had subdued." In the words of St Paul, "having wiped out the handwriting of requirements that was against us, which was contrary to us. And He has taken it out of the way, having nailed it to the cross. Having disarmed principalities and powers, He made a public spectacle of them, triumphing over them in it," (Col 2:14-15).

The Jews taunted and tortured Him in order to hear from Him a protest or a cry for help but He kept silent. He was distressed but did not complain and so they were shattered, vanquished and mortified saying, "If You are the Son of God, come down from the cross," (Matt27:39). If He had come down from the cross, there would have been no salvation for mankind and they would not have believed in Him, just as they had not believed those who had witnessed the raising of Lazarus from death. Christ's choice not to save Himself though He was able is a greater marvel than would have been had He chosen to save Himself from death. He did not accept death through helplessness or compulsion but rather by His own will. Opinions differ on the event in Christ's life through which He was most glorified, some say it was His transfiguration, others His walking upon the water or some of His miracles, nothing, however, glorified the Son of God as much as His death. When Judas left Him in order to deliver Him up to the Jews Jesus said, "Now the Son of Man is glorified," (Jn 13:31). For glory is not determined by the wearing of fine apparel or by the sitting on lofty thrones, but rather by the accomplishment of the will of God.

So Christ did triumph but through weakness not strength and through poverty not wealth. Has it ever happened in the history of mankind that the weak prevailed over the strong, the poor over the wealthy and the dead over the living?

Rejoice and be glad you sinners while Jesus sorrows, for His sorrow is your joy. Sing a song of victory as He lowers His head for He bows to raise you. Now you have attained your wishes. Jesus has died for you. Does this news gladden you?

Do you wish to ascertain the matter for yourselves? Come and see the wounds that have congealed all over His pure body because of your transgressions, witness His crushed and gashed body hanging on the cross because of the deluge of your lusts, His head aching from the sting of your conceit and His lips bitter from the poison of your blasphemous tongue.

It is said of King Seleucus that he sat on the seashore, after being deposed, and as the waves washed over him, his enemies approached him, thinking to rejoice at the sight of him in such a miserable state. When they found him, however, sitting on the sand, fearful, naked, shaking from the cold and bereft of all hope, their hearts were softened toward him despite themselves and they had so much compassion they lifted him up and restored him to his throne in honour.

Will you do the same o mankind? Your sins have been ascribed to your God and have made Him descend from the throne of His glory to the cross of shame, and today we see Him flung upon the cross without comforter or helper in a state to make even an enemy weep. Has your heart softened toward Him? Have you resolved to leave your sins that He may return to His throne glorified and joyful? Even Christ's scourger's and crucifiers, after they had tortured Him, descended the hill ashamed of the severity of the torture and moved by the immensity of His patience, as it is written, "And the whole crowd who came together to that sight, seeing what had been done, beat their breasts and returned," (Lk:23:48). Is the cruelty of our hearts so much greater than that of those witnessed or caused His death? Do we love sin to the extent that we allow it to eliminate all concern for Him who suffered so much for our sakes?

If one sees another miserable, will he not feel compassion toward him though he is a stranger? Christ, however, is no stranger - He is our Creator, our Saviour, our Benefactor and the bearer of our afflictions! His condition reproaches us saying, "Why do you gaze upon My cross without offering a look of compassion or a word of tenderness, though pity yourselves soon enough when you cannot partake of your lusts and sins? Why do you not shed a single tear for Me though everyday you shed copious tears for your loved ones, your relations and even for your lost money?"

Let us examine ourselves and confess that it was for our sakes, contemptible creatures that we are, that He accepted all this suffering. No other reason compelled Him but His desire to proclaim His love for us. Let us observe ourselves in this lucid mirror to correct our conduct and to demonstrate toward Him the esteem and glory of affection and an appreciation of the favour bestowed. Let our hearts be rent with sorrow and regret for we have displeased our good God. Let us love Him Who has loved us beyond measure. Although the death of the Son of God is a concept beyond the understanding of humankind, it is imperative for us to know why He died. He died for man's wickedness and his salvation from sin as shown by St Paul, "For I delivered to you first of all that which I also received: that Christ died for our sins according to the Scriptures," (I Cor 15:3).

As one of the fathers contemplated, "As for You, the crucified One who looks down from the heights of Golgotha, Your dignity and majesty far exceeds that of a thousand kings seated on a thousand thrones in a thousand kingdoms, though You hang from a cross steeped in Your blood. You are more fearsome and formidable than a thousand commanders leading a thousand armies on a thousand battles, even in those last moments before Your death. You are more joyful in Your grief than the spring with its abundant flowers. In Your suffering, You are more serene than the angels in their heavens are. You are freer in the hands of Your abusers than the radiance of the Sun. The crown of thorns on Your head is more majestic and beautiful than a bejewelled royal crown and the nail in Your hand more precious than a royal sceptre. The drops of blood on Your feet are more brilliant than the jewels of Ashtoreth".

Cast down upon us, O blessed Son of God, from the heights of Your cross - a look of pity and compassion for our corrupted nature, not a look of anger and pain due to our hard hearts. Veil Your eyes from seeing our offence, O Jesus, so that You do not crush us but rather look upon our miserable condition and raise us up in Your power and love.

As the children of Israel lifted their eyes to the rock Moses struck to bring forth water, so we lift our eyes to the holy cross of Jesus, over which flowed blood and water from the Saviour's side as the Psalmist says, "And with honey from the rock I would have satisfied you," (Ps 81:16). As for us, we seek from You bitter water in return for that drunk by our Representative to You, for we seek to grieve over His pain and mourn over His torture. Not only over His pain and torture but also over our sins that are the cause of all this suffering, and that we still cling to as if wanting our Saviour to perpetually suffer on our behalf.

Look, O my eyes, upon Him crucified and listen, O my ears, to the hammer, pounding the nails into my Beloveds' body. Taste O my tongue, the bitterness that He, of whom it was said, "His mouth is most sweet, Yes, He is altogether lovely," (Song of Sol 5:16), tasted before you. Contemplate, O my soul, the extent to which your God has gone for you. He enthroned Himself upon the cross, assumed a crown of thorns, robed Himself with nakedness and accepted nails for His royal sceptre and sour wine and gall for His drink. Should you not then mourn and weep for your negligence in your service to Him? Here He is humiliated and insulted for your sake! Does this not shatter your conceit and weaken your pride?

Who am I, my perfect Saviour that You should die for me? You whose glory the angels desire to glimpse? What is my worth that you should pay such an exorbitant price for me. For one drop, of Your precious blood, is worth much more than heaven and earth and all that is in them. My Lord, my soul is so valuable in Your eyes though worthless in my own, because I underestimate it and do not offer it to You but instead offer it upon the altar of the lust of the eyes and pride of life (I Jn 2:16).

Here I am now, my God, so thrust into my eyes the thorns of

Your crown that they may purify and sanctify all they look upon. Fill my ears with the blasphemies directed at You that they may not revert to listening to this world's vain words. Allow my mouth taste to drink of the bitterness You tasted so that it will no longer utter lies. How I grieve that I am unable to bear the slightest burden for Your sake, You has borne the most intense pain on my behalf in order to save me from suffering. You accepted death to grant me life. You put on my body that You may adorn me with Your Holy Spirit. You have carried my sins upon Your shoulders, in order to endow me with Your grace. Grant me to consider suffering for Your sake my strength, deprivation my prosperity and death my life. Allow me to regard Your suffering as my treasure, Your crown of thorns as my glory, Your pain my consolation, as the bitterness You tasted as my sweetness, Your wounds as my wellbeing, Your blood as my life and Your love as my pride and joy.

But how, my Saviour, can I thank You for this Your love for me and how can I repay You for all the pain and suffering You endured for my sake? If I could offer You the whole world and if I accepted all pain borne by thousands of generations, I would still be unable to repay all my debt to You. I am, therefore, indebted to You eternally and it is well for me to be indebted to You. You are glorified by the Father and by Your angels, and all Your creation perpetually praises You. But I am very weak and feeble and so grant, my good Saviour, that I may sense Your grace at all times.

CHAPTER 7

Jesus Alone

"I have trodden the winepress alone, And from the peoples
no one was with Me" (Isa 63:3)

With the eyes of prophecy, the prophet sees a man who appears to be coming out of a great struggle, and wearing a garment so covered in blood that it appears to be scarlet in colour, and so he asks Him, "Who are You?", and He answers, "I am the one who has 'trodden the winepress alone'" (Isa 63:3).

How strongly this prophecy alludes to the atoning work of Christ in that He came down to this world alone, unaccompanied by any of His angelic host. He has trodden the garden of sorrow alone and drunk the cup of suffering, even the dregs, with no one to share it with Him. He has ascended the wood of the cross on His own, abandoned by every comforter and helper, as evident in His mournful cry for help, "I looked for someone to take pity, but there was none; And for comforters, but I found none," (Ps 69:20).

'I have trodden the winepress alone'. An expression that is pleasant only in the mouth of Christ, and musical to the ears only when uttered by Him. For can anyone, whether an angel or a man, walk the way of the cross but Jesus? Who can pass through that forbidding trail without the least comfort from a friend? The martyrs in the midst of their tortures were comforted by the blessed name of Christ, but the beloved Son was alone in His afflictions and without equal in His suffering. On the mount of the Transfiguration, Moses and Elijah appeared and spoke with Him about His impending suffering, but when the disciples asked for them to remain with Him, they disappeared and "Jesus was found alone," (Lk 9:34), as an indication that He would be alone in the work of Salvation on the mount of Golgotha.

We will never find, in the history of mankind, that all people from all ranks and walks of life were united together against one man. For if it happens that a government rises against him some people will be found to defend him or conversely, or if persecuted by the rich he will be accepted by the poor. Which man, if treated unjustly by some will not find compassion with others? When King Ahab persecuted Elijah, a widow in Zarephath provided for him, and when David was rejected by Saul, foreign kings aided him, and when Jeremiah the prophet was cast into a dungeon by his own people a Cushite man was found to show him compassion.

Against our Lord Jesus Christ alone all conspired, and He alone did not receive the least compassion from a single person. Atheists, Jews - priests, lay people, lawyers, soldiers and elders, Romans - plebeians, senators, and magistrates, the old and young, the simple and wicked, the hypocrites, the believers and the non believers and the idol worshippers, as the Psalm foretold, "Many bulls encompass Me; strong bulls of Bashan have encircled Me.... They gape at Me with their mouths, Like a raging and roaring lion..... For dogs have surrounded Me; The congregation of the wicked has enclosed Me," (Ps 22:12, 13, 16).

Why do you masters all scheme against Him is not He the One who commanded the slaves to honour you? Why have you slaves persecuted Him - did He not ask your masters to be gentle with you? And you priests, why have you hated Him when He was the One who honoured your rank and dignified your authority? Why have you resisted Him, you Pharisees - has He not commanded your principles to be obeyed? Why have you tax collectors shown Him hostility when they persecuted Him for accepting you? You people, why have you turned against Him when He spent all His time showing you kindness – teaching the ignorant, encouraging the fearful, comforting the downhearted, healing the sick and feeding the hungry? Why have you eminent citizens opposed Him when He has never envied you your honour and glory, and you miserly, why have you conspired against Him when He has never asked you for your silver or gold? Why did you not take His side you judicious while He commands all to pursue wisdom, and why did you not stand by Him you sinners though He alone of all people sought compassion for you? It has been in truth said, "Those who hate me without a cause are more than the hairs of my head," (Ps: 69:4).

Many times when a death sentence is passed down, it is very difficult to find someone who is ready and willing to carry out this atrocity, but when Jesus was condemned to death by crucifixion, many people were eager to be involved in His torture and injury.

When the subjects of King Charles executed him in Whitehall, they wore masks because of the disgrace of being identified. The executioners of Jesus, on the other hand, boasted that they were all His enemies, as was prophesied in the Psalm, "For behold, Your enemies make a tumult; And those who hate You have lifted up their head," (Ps 83:2).

How great our Saviour's sorrow must have been when He found Himself alone in the midst of His great affliction, shown no compassion from those toward whom He had previously shown compassion and benevolence. Where were all the blind whose eyes Jesus had opened? Where were the lame, the maimed, the mute, and the deaf whom Jesus healed? Where were the tax collectors whom He had accepted? Where were the mournful He had comforted? Not one of these was by His side in His distress or adversity.

It is the hardest thing for a man that his act of kindness

is denied at his time of need. When Christ was crucified, not one of those He had healed came to Him to console Him or to ease His suffering with a tender word. There is no doubt that many of those healed through the miracles of Christ and other beneficiaries of His kindness were in Jerusalem for the feast of the Passover. How, then, did they react when the mob rose against Christ and began to curse and mock Him? Were any of them moved by gallantry enough to protest against the clamour with the words, "Desist from your blasphemies and say nothing against the crucified One for His kindness toward me has been supreme"?

Christ was condemned to death and there was not found one to defend Him nor to protest against or question Pilate's judgment.

No doubt there were, present in Jerusalem, some of the five thousand who along with their wives and children, were fed by Him with five loaves of bread and two fish. No doubt too there were in the crowd the blind man who received his sight, the deaf who was healed of his deafness, the mute who was given speech, the paralytic who was made to walk, the lepers who were cleansed, the demon-possessed who was healed, and the dead who were raised. Where are Jairus and his daughter? Where are the widow of Nain and her son? Where are Lazarus and his two sisters? Suppose that these all were a part of the general populace and did not dare to utter a word before the authorities who crucified Him, What about all the prominent people whom Christ had embraced like Joseph of Aramithea, Nicodemus teacher of the law and the centurion whose servant Jesus healed? Not one of these made even the slightest attempt to help the Saviour. He would have rejoiced, even with a failed attempt, knowing that some had acknowledged His goodness and appreciated His benevolence.

Indeed all who were blessed by Him used His goodness to magnify His suffering and His anguish. No doubt that, from amongst His crucifiers, were recipients of His benevolence, as one elder contemplated, "Among them were those whose hands were healed by Him yet in His time of suffering they stretched out their hands to pull His holy hair, and those who received healing of their limp legs, but used them to kick Him, and still others who taunted and blasphemed Him with the same tongues that once were tied but were loosened by the divine might of Jesus. On some He had bestowed the gift of life and yet in the midst of His agony they drove Him to the mount to be crucified. They exceeded all bounds by denying the benevolence of Jesus and abusing Him by means of the very gifts He had granted them through His divine mercy and thereby fulfilling the words of the prophet, "They reward me evil for good, to the sorrow of my soul," (Ps 35:12).

Where, also, were His disciples whom He had overwhelmed with His grace? Why did they not follow Him carrying the cross? Where was Thomas who had said, "Let us also go, that we may die with Him," (Jn 11:16)? What does the Bible say concerning the disciples at the time of Jesus' arrest? "Then all the disciples forsook Him and fled," (Matt 26:56). Indeed His own words, "the hour is coming, yes, has now come, that you will be scattered, each to his own, and will leave Me alone," (Jn 16:32), and "All of you will be made to stumble because of Me this night, for it is written: `I will strike the Shepherd, And the sheep of the flock will be scattered'," (Matt 26:31) were realized.

Now the Good Shepherd has been struck, and the sheep have fled leaving their Shepherd in the hands of wolves. Where is your zeal Peter, when you said, "Even if all are made to stumble because of You, I will never be made to stumble. ... Even if I have to die with You, I will not deny You! And so said all the disciples," (Matt 26:33, 35). You Disciples of Christ, why are you not true to your words? Where is your love John? Where is Andrew who was the first among them to be called? Where is Matthew whom He had restored from the error of his ways? Where are all the rest who had received such abundant goodness and enjoyed such bounty?

It was reprehensible that those, who were His companions and had witnessed all His amazing miracles, had also fled away - those who had beheld Him raising the dead, opening the eyes of the blind, healing the sick, feeding the multitudes with a few loaves of bread, walking on water and the winds and calming the raging waves and storms. Have you forgotten all these things so that you would run away? Has your memory of the power and might, that Christ had made so evident before you, faded so quickly, or have you fled so that He would tread the winepress alone?

As someone had contemplated, "When a person is bed-ridden, he is surrounded by parents, friends and physicians who will offer comfort and amusement alongside his bitter medication. Jesus, however, in the midst of His anguish could not find one to comfort or console Him. Would He ask for Peter who denies Him or John who follows Him at a distance, or Judas who has sold Him? Would He ask for His angels when His Father has turned His face away? Would He seek the rich who are preoccupied with their wealth or the distinguished preoccupied with their glory? Job was comforted in his suffering by his friends, Naaman received for his leprosy solace and healing from Elijah, and Daniel was visited in the den by an angel, but Christ could not find a judge to vindicate Him, an angel to comfort Him, nor a friend to console and relieve Him ."

Only You Lord could not find, in Your afflictions, a single word of comfort nor one of encouragement to help You bear the shame of the cross. Sadly You gazed about You at the height of Your pain as if to say, "I looked, but there was no one to help, And I wondered That there was no one to uphold," (Isa 63:5).

In the words of one of the fathers, "Who will comfort You, O Second Adam, sent from the paradise of Jerusalem to Moriah the desolate mountain. Who will soothe You Joseph whom they sold, the suffering Job, the persecuted Daniel, the oppressed Isaiah and the mournful Elijah. We fear lest in approaching You thus we may add to Your suffering that was caused by our sins for it is not possible for the source of one's distress to also be that of its comfort and succour. Be blessed then O Son of God.

Be comforted by the fruits the tree of Your cross have yielded. Let the salvation, you have wrought for the entire world be Your consolation. Be comforted, O Noah, for by being inundated by a sea of agony, You save sinners through the ark of Your holy church. Be comforted, O Joseph, for You will emerge from the prison of oppression to reign over Your Father's kingdom forever. Be comforted O Job, for Your ordeals have broadcast Your glory. Be comforted O Daniel, for You will be lifted up from the lion's den, to the throne of Your majesty."

And now what have we resolved to do? Maybe we are determined to denounce those who abandoned Christ their benefactor, yet have we not perceived that we behave in the same way? Christ, even now, sits on His throne at the right of His Father yearning to present to His Father children who have acknowledged His grace and appreciated His favour in dying on their behalf, as noted by the Apostle Paul, "For it was fitting for Him, for whom are all things and by whom are all things, in bringing many sons to glory, to make the captain of their salvation perfect through sufferings," (Heb 2:10). So do we then flee, deserting Him and refusing to offer ourselves up to Him to honour Him before His Father? The delight of the Son, and His glory before the Father, is the salvation of many. The prophet Isaiah wrote, "He shall see the labour of His soul, and be satisfied," (Isa 53:11). So faithfully submitting ourselves to Christ in order for Him to present us to His Father, is His pleasure and rest, just as our forsaking and abandoning Him, His grief and sorrow. Shall we leave Him alone before His Father, just as His friends did at the cross? In our perception, their offense is great for they abandoned Him who showed them such grace. The grace He has shown us, however, is far greater for He had not as yet died on their behalf, granted them the blessings of heaven, nor poured upon them His Holy Spirit.

We must be aware that those who abandon the Son of God will themselves be abandoned at their time of need. Those who had deserted Him He has received when they have came back to Him, for He had not asked nor encouraged any of them to accompany Him to the cross and they had fled because they had not known what would eventuate. Now, however, those who flee and abandon Him, will themselves be abandoned by Him in their time of need, for it was for them He had come forth with His cross, death, resurrection and Holy Spirit and whom He had asked to accompany Him that He may present them to His Father.

Let us then submit ourselves to Him in obedience that He may present us to His Father saying, "Here am I and the children whom God has given Me," (Heb 2:13) and also, "Those whom You gave Me I have kept; and none of them is lost," (Jn 17:12).

CHAPTER 8

Jesus Wounded in the House of His Friends

"And one will say to him, 'What are these wounds between your arms?'
Then he will answer, 'Those with which I was wounded in the house of my
friends'" (Zech 13:6)

This is astonishing! Is love cruel? Does it persecute? Does it wound? Does it crucify? Love suffers long and is kind. It is not easily angered. So then, why do we hear today that the wounds were suffered in the house of friends and how then are the hearts hardened against the beloved? It is because envy transforms love to enmity, "the chief priests had handed Him over because of envy," (Mk 15:10).

Why was there such loathing for the Beloved and why such envy? It was because He is righteous and they were evil, and darkness cannot concur with the Light. His righteousness exposed their vileness just as the sun, when it rises, reveals all the filth on the earth. In this way, the pure life of Jesus reproached their corruption and iniquities. As David's presence and goodness was the cause of Saul's misery, so the holy presence of Jesus distressed the wicked amongst the people.

They hated Him because He was faithful in His love. Jesus knows how repulsive sin is and how great its punishment and yet saw how they clung to it. As a Beloved who desires to save His loved ones from harm and to rescue them from danger, He warned them against sin. Had He kept silent and not rebuked them for their hypocrisy, they would not have hated Him. Had He deceived them they would have honoured Him, but because He was faithful they detested Him, for people hate the truth, though it may emanate from the mouth of a friend, and love falsehood though the source may be an adversary, as St Paul observed, "Have I therefore become your enemy because I tell you the truth?" (Gal 4:16).

The Saviour's wounds remained visible on His body after the resurrection that all may be astonished when they consider what His loved ones inflicted upon their Beloved. the prophet foretold,

"And one will say to him, 'What are these wounds between your arms?' Then he will answer, 'Those with which I was wounded in the house of my friends.'" (Zech 13:6). A loved one binds and does not wound. Whenever I remember that my wounds were caused by My loved ones my pain is renewed and my sorrow is intensified.

Let us now contemplate the following:

A. That the difficulty of a trial will depend on its source.

Is it not the case that in many instances an ordeal would have gone unnoticed had it come from a different source? If an enemy mocks us, we may not pay much attention, but if a valued friend offends us we will very much resent his attack and scorn. Every wound grieves us, but that which a friend inflicts is very painful and penetrates as an arrow to the heart.

The Psalmist ponders, "For it is not an enemy who reproaches me; Then I could bear it. Nor is it one who hates me who has exalted himself against me; Then I could hide from him. But it was you, a man my equal, My companion and my acquaintance. We took sweet counsel together," (Ps 55:12-14).

It is said of Julius Caesar, the great Roman Emperor, that his senators had conspired against him to kill him out of envy, and amongst them was Brutus, his closest friend whom he had promoted to the highest rank. It happened, on that fateful day, that once they had lured him into the courts, they shut the doors and drew out their swords and daggers. He valiantly defended himself but when he saw Brutus attacking him holding a dagger to stab him, he was greatly grieved by his betrayal. It was then that he uttered those famous words of reproach, "You too, Brutus!" After which he ceased to defend himself and fell to the ground in a pool of blood.

In this way, the Lord's sorrows intensified whenever He saw, amongst His slayers and crucifiers, those to whom He had granted blessings and supported and for whom He had borne such hardships, even more so when He saw that the creation for which He came to die itself condemned Him to this very death.

I.   "wounded by His friends," – because the creation He had covered with His glory and honour has abused, despised and stripped Him naked. The earth He had created has produced thorns for Him to be crowned with and wood to be crucified upon. Indeed God has granted His creation every good thing and in return, it has offered evil. He bestows it with grace and it finds nothing at hand with which to repay Him apart from transgression and corruption. He fed the multitude in the wilderness after blessing the loaves with His pure hands and in return, it satiates Him with taunts and holds out to Him swords and spears in place of food. He quenched them with superior wine at the wedding of Cana of Galilee but in His thirst they lifted up to Him gall and offered Him sour wine. He cast out their demons and they called him the chief of demons. He restored their sinners and they called him a transgressor though He is the holy and righteous. He raised their dead and gave them life and they slaughtered Him upon the cross.

The rebellious creatures perceived good as evil. Pilate had asked them, "What evil has He done?", and they found none. They responded that He had opened the eyes of the blind, cleansed lepers, healed the lame and the paralysed on the Sabbath. They wished to vilify Him but instead praised Him. Thus people, at all times, suppose God's blessings to be detrimental. Who, when they contemplate this hideous deed by mankind against its Creator, would fail to be greatly astonished, especially if they think upon the goodness He has bestowed them and the evil with which they have repaid Him. He honoured them but they abused Him. He performed mighty acts but they blasphemed Him. He cured their sick but they tortured Him. He indulged them with His goodness but they drowned Him in the abyss of their transgressions. The physician who visited them with healing was wounded for His trouble. They planted sharp thorns in His compassionate head and caused it to bleed. They carried swords and sticks against Him who bound their wounds, healed them and showed them His benevolence.

Yes, they stretched the hands that had reached out to them with an offer of salvation and had faithfully borne gifts and healing. They pierced the feet that had ventured toward them in order to ease their afflictions and to take away their grief. They emerged as enemies before the eyes that had shed hot and bitter tears on their behalf. The ears that had compassionately heard their sighs they deafened with their profanities and cursing. They made the mouth bitter that had uttered words of wisdom, blessing and comfort. They wounded the heart that had pitied them, broke it from shame and cast it into an inferno until it melted as wax. He revealed to them His side full of kindness and mercy and they pierced it with spears. Thus the prophecy was fulfilled, "In return for my love they are my accusers, But I give myself to prayer. Thus they have rewarded me evil for good, And hatred for my love," (Ps 109:4-5).

O you ungrateful and thankless creation, why do you look at Me as you would an enemy, while I am the source of all benevolence? At the very moment in which you rise against Me you are basking in all I have endowed you with. You speak mocking words and mouth blasphemous expressions while I prepare for your mouths sustenance and for your tongues noble words. I keep you from all the danger and you conspire against Me. With which hand do you slap Me? Is it not with the same hand that I created for you? With which tongue do you blaspheme me and with which eyes do you look at Me with such contempt and with which feet have you hurried in order to crucify Me? Am I not the one who fashioned for you all these members and gave you all these senses? Everywhere and at all times many have abused these gifts and rather than serving Me with them have delivered them to the adversary and caused them to be instruments in the hands of Satan to use against Me.

2. "wounded by His friends," – because the Jewish nation, which He had kept close to Himself from its inception, had hated Him by loving its enemies. It had loved the hated Caesar to be free of Jesus! It had allied itself to the Roman Empire in order to have Him killed and had forcefully demanded of Pilate to "crucify Him, crucify Him". Do these words come from the same mouth that has eaten manna in the wilderness and quails in the desert, the mouth that has tasted milk and honey in the Promised Land, the mouth that should have been offering up thanks to Him Who had been so good to it? Do you raise your voice up

in shouts of revenge and cries of enmity? Do you thus scorn the God Who had honoured and dignified you with abundant gifts and blessings. To this extent do you offend your Saviour who has favoured you above all nations and chosen you over them?

St Jacob of Serug said, "See how the Jewish nations had committed adultery, despised its Father and detested Him at Sinai. Then when the Son was incarnate for its salvation, they took hold of Him and laid Him upon the cross, then stood by dancing, laughing, deriding and mocking. Come Moses and behold what the bride, you brought out of Egypt, has done to her holy Bridegroom? Come and see the banquet she has placed before Him: she has prepared gall and mixed sour wine in return for the Manna and pleasant water. The chosen vine has yielded rotten grapes."

O you cruel race, do you condemn Jesus the benevolent to death? Is He not the One Who has loved you with all His heart and soul? What is this I hear you say? "The governor answered and said to them, Which of the two do you want me to release to you? They said, Barabbas! Pilate said to them, What then shall I do with Jesus who is called Christ? They all said to him, Let Him be crucified!"

(Matt 27: 21-22). "The God of Abraham, Isaac, and Jacob, the God of our fathers, glorified His Servant Jesus, whom you delivered up and denied in the presence of Pilate, when he was determined to let Him go. But you denied the Holy One and the Just, and asked for a murderer to be granted to you, and killed the Prince of life," (Act 3:13-15).

How astonishing! You ask for the life of Barabbas the assassin and condemn to death compassionate Jesus! Is not the Lord the

One Who preformed wonders in Egypt for your sake? Is He not the One who took you out of Egypt with a mighty hand? Is He not the One who has bestowed upon you all goodness? Did Barabbas open the eyes of your blind? Did he cure your sick, cleanse your lepers or raise your dead? How I lament Your grief O beloved Son of God, when I see this Your chosen and beloved nation rise and harden itself against You and prefer the outlaw over You. This, though, is the very deed sinners do at all times. Every day they honour creation more than the Creator, they demand hell and desire it, they abandon heaven and neglect it, they seek honour from the world rather than from God. In the world of Barabbas is found the wealth, honour, pride, adultery, intoxication, conflict and all evil that you still desire and cling to, you wretched sinner, while you forsake your good share Jesus Christ.

3. "wounded by His friends," – because Judas, His disciple and treasurer, betrayed Him and sold Him for a mere thirty pieces of silver of coin. Look at him cunningly approaching Jesus, along with some soldiers in order to give Him up to them, saying, "Greetings, Rabbi!" (Matt: 26:49) and kissing Him. O what a poisoned tongue and O what treacherous lips! "Are you betraying the Son of Man with a kiss?" (Lk 22:48). What a horrid display of ingratitude, O monstrous and cruel heart! Did His sweet words not move you? Did His amazing miracles not convince you? Indeed when the lust of the world enters the heart, it renders it blind even to the most brilliant light.

Hear the Saviour saying to him, "Friend, why have you come?" (Matt 26:50). He calls him friend, and God extends friendship to all mankind His and blesses them with His favour, "for He makes His sun rise on the evil and on the good, and sends rain on the just and on the unjust," (Matt 5:45). My friend, how can you deny my goodness toward you? Is this how you reward Me Judas? Am I not the One who fed you My bread? How then can you lift your heel against Me? (Ps 41:9).

Do you deliver these hands that have washed your feet to be bound? Is this the gratitude I expected from you? I would have preferred to be crowned with a thousand crowns of thorns, and to be pierced with a thousand spears rather than being kissed in this way or witnessing such treason. One of the fathers said, "An outward gesture of peace, but a concealed extended sword. Fear, O people, the deceitful kiss, for with one the Son of God was hanged on the wood of the cross!"

4. "wounded by His friends," – because Peter, His disciple and known for his zeal, denied and disowned Him. When the Lord perceived that Peter was denying Him He looked at him (Lk 22:60, 61). What was the meaning behind that look? Did it not break his heart? Did it not burn his bowels, melt his emotions and inflame all his senses? He looked at him as if to say, "Where is the courage you boasted of? Where are your promises? Only hours before you were vowing that even if you had to die with Me you would not deny Me and now you swear that you know Me not. Were you not the one who witnessed that I am the Christ, the Son of God? The mouth that had confessed Me to be the Son of God now denies association with Me. Am I not the One who enabled you to walk on water, and when you were on the verge of drowning, did I not snatch you up? Why then, Peter, do you leave Me to sink alone in the abyss of suffering?

5. "wounded by His friends," – because John followed Him from afar (Mk 14:50). And who is John? He is the disciple renowned for being beloved of Christ. The beloved stands far away like a stranger. Do you fear that they will recognise you as one of Mine? The disciples believed you to be supremely close to Me, so close that on the night of the Passover, they dared not question Me except through you. Why do you now not come near, and why do you refrain from manifesting yourself?

6. "wounded by His friends," – because all His disciples left Him and fled. Why do you flee? Do you fear the harm or dread the shame? Is this what was expected from you in the hour of need, that you should abandon the Beloved in the time of His suffering? How can the sheep leave their shepherd and run off while He makes them lie down in green pastures and leads them beside the still waters.

Here is great comfort for all those whose friends have betrayed them. Do not be saddened or dejected for Jesus was betrayed by all His friends first. He is able to comfort us and support us when we traverse the same difficult road that ends in ingratitude.

He is able to comfort us in all our tribulation, because being tempted He is able to aid those who are tempted.

B. Does the Beloved deserve such cruelty from His loved ones?

The Master came to the house of His loved ones carrying the banner of peace, extending hands full of approbation, grace and compassion, ready to bear all hardship for the sake of their repose. The Master's loved ones, however, whom He sought and approached would not receive Him have closed the door in His face. "He came to His own, and His own did not receive Him," (John 1:11). They not only rejected Him but also wounded Him with deep wounds and stood before Him cursing as was prophesied, "My loved ones and my friends stand aloof from my plague, And my relatives stand afar off," (Ps 38:11) and "They have also surrounded me with words of hatred, And fought against me without a cause," (Ps 109:3).

Did Jesus then deserve all this from His beloved? He had left His glory, had shared in their human nature and was tempted in every way like them. While they treated him with cruelty and harshness, He sighed and wept for them. "They reward Me evil for good to the sorrow of My soul. But as for me, when they were sick, My clothing was sackcloth; ... I bowed down heavily, as one who mourns for his mother. But in my adversity they rejoiced And gathered together; Attackers gathered against me, And I did not know it," (Ps 35:12-15). If anyone had passed Him by and had seen Him hanging on the cross, they would have cried out to Him asking, "What are these wounds in Your hand?" and He would then answer, "These are the wounds I received in the house of My beloved." Indeed He was condemned to death in the house of the High Priest (Matt 26:57, 27:1).

If He had been asked, "Had You harmed them, Lord, that they should wound You?" the answer would have been, "No, for they themselves had conceded, 'He has done all things well. He makes both the deaf to hear and the mute to speak' (Mk 7:37), and My deeds have been deeds of kindness, compassion, mercy and love.

"How often I wanted to gather your children together, as a

hen gathers her chicks under her wings," (Matt 23:37). Despite this they treated Me as they would an enemy. They rewarded the goodness of My grace with wickedness and malevolence, so that the prophecy concerning Me may be fulfilled, "I have become a stranger to my brothers, And an alien to my mother's children," (Ps 69:8).

Indeed Jesus was able to save Himself, but He accepted, with gladness, all these wounds in His holy body in order to procure salvation for us. What then is greater than His love for us, and what is more atrocious than our enmity toward Him.

C. What do we learn from all these happenings?

Had you been present at the time of the Christ's crucifixion, what would you have done? You say, no doubt I would have done my utmost to prevent my Lord's suffering. This is good, but do you not realise that, even now you wound Him more severely than He was wounded at the hands of the Jews. They wounded Him in ignorance, but you have deliberately wounded Him with your evil conduct even after the fact of His suffering and death on your behalf. Your conduct is abominable, you immerse yourself in depravity, you mar the image God had engraved in you, you are boastful, proud, cruel, lazy in fulfilling your obligations toward your God, church and self and you deceive yourself concerning the truth. Do you not know that by doing all this you leave yourself open to the realm of sin, obliterating the voice of your conscience, despising counsel, heedless of advice, unconcerned by instruction and warning? Do you not know that all this has a more atrocious and hideous effect upon the merciful Prince of Peace the Lord Jesus Christ?

Beware, O man, and ponder what the Creator has granted you and how you have repaid. Your God died and arose bearing the marks of His wounds in His head, hands, feet and side as proof of His love and faithfulness to mankind. One of the fathers contemplated, "The Saviour opens His side to us that we may see the extent of the love He carries in His heart for us and that the sinner may enter and wash away his sins. He offers His pierced hands and feet that it may be apparent that His love is available to all sinners no matter their sin, even those who have crucified and killed Him. With His wounded hands, He approaches His Father seeking pardon for those who wounded Him. With His benevolent mouth, that tasted bitterness, He announces remission of the sins of those who meted out that bitterness. From His side that was pierced with a spear, blood pours forth to purify the one who pierced Him. He leaves this side and these wounds open to this day that there may be, for you O sinner, remedy for your sins and comfort your pain."

Jesus declares as in the words of St. Ambrose, "Know that these wounds teach you that, in every time and place, I am a healing Physician to all who are wounded, and to those who are inflamed by sin, I am the Spring that quenches its flame. To the oppressed, I will be Justice and fairness and to the weak and helpless, Strength and Support. To those who fear death, I will be Life, and to those who love heaven, the Way. To those who flee darkness, I will be Light, and to the hungry, Sustenance."

It is for the love of you, O man, Jesus was wounded, and for it, He retains them. So, glory in the fact that you have a Master such as this, wounded for your love and preserving His wounds not only to expose man's infidelity, but also to motivate man to return to his first love.

For the wounds of Jesus are as many tongues calling sinners back to Him. For the privilege of these wounds then, do not persist in your sins, and continue in your wickedness. For the hand that was pierced is ready to hold your hands and to guide you in the path of righteousness. The feet that were nailed to the cross are ready to strive with you to bring you to the way of salvation. The eyes that wept from pain look to all with compassion, affection and kindness. The ears that were filled with abuse, always heed the calls of those who seek His succour.

Consider what benefit the Jews gained from their cruelty, what profit they obtained from not repenting, and whether the wounds diminished the Beloved's worth. He who wounds others wounds, only wounds himself. "Whoever digs a pit will fall into it, And he who rolls a stone will have it roll back on him," (Prov 26:27). When the Jews gored the crucified One, they gored themselves, and when they crowned Him with a crown of thorns, they entwined for their heads a crown of shame forever. As for Christ, He is risen victoriously from death. Sin clings to those that love it, shame adheres to its friends, and oppression has returned upon its perpetrators.

For the sin you commit against Jesus, does not disparage nor hurt Him, but affects Him because it emanates from people He loved and died for, "for whatever a man sows, that he will also reap," (Gal 6:7).

Christ is victorious at all the times. Indeed, he is risen maintaining the marks of His wounds, but their pain has vanished. These visible wounds become a witness against those who would persist in their sin and would show no contrition, "They shall look on Him whom they pierced," (Jn 19:37). "Behold, He is coming with clouds, and every eye will see Him, even they who pierced Him. And all the tribes of the earth will mourn because of Him," (Rev 1:7).

Then they "said to the mountains and rocks, Fall on us and hide us from the face of Him who sits on the throne and from the wrath of the Lamb!" (Rev 6:16). Hide us O mountains lest our eyes should see the wounds that are clearly evident on His body as a sign of His love for us, while we exhibit on our own signs of our enmity toward Him. In His body is proof of His compassion upon us and in ours proof of cruelty against Him.

O my God, the traces of bitterness in your mouth is proof of Your love for us, and the foul language in ours proof of hatred. The wound marks on Your hands and feet, are evidence of Your compassion for us, but our sin-filled hands and our fickle feet, evidence of the cruelty of our hearts. The tears that have filled Your eyes over our sins, is a banner of Your mercy, but the depravity of our eyes indicates our unworthiness of this abundant mercy.

O Lord, You extend Your hands to bestow blessing, while our hands are lifted up in sin. With Your mouth You edify us, but with ours we blaspheme You. With Your ears You heed our cries, but we fill ours with foolishness. Your eyes look upon distress and You save us, while ours perceive evil and lust after it and iniquity and longs for it. You bow Your head while our sins crowned it with thorns, though ours are lifted up in conceit and disdain. Your heart melts as a candle before a flame as You pursue our salvation, while ours love the world without You esteeming sin over You. O holy Son of God, cleanse our hands so we may offer you the fruits of godliness. Purify our lips that they may give You thanks unceasingly. Bless our eyes that they may see only You. Fill our hearts with Your love, and let our ears exult only in hearing Your sweet voice. Bow our heads before Your glory, take us totally to be

Your own, and do not allow any other reign over us.

You faithful people ponder these wounds through which we attained righteousness and healing. Let us place them always before us, forbidding Satan or any other power from making us forget them. Let us rather remember them forever and inscribe them upon the pages of our hearts, for with them we have been saved from all our sins.

CHAPTER 9

Nature Witnesses to Jesus

"Now when the sixth hour had come, there was darkness over
the whole land until the ninth hour" (Mk 15:33)

"Then, behold, the veil of the temple was torn in two from top to bottom; and the earth quaked, and the rocks were split, and the graves were opened; and many bodies of the saints who had fallen asleep were raised," (Matt 27:51, 52).

Mankind crucified its Creator! They claimed He was a criminal and justified themselves. Consequently, nature rose up to justify Him and to condemn them.

It observed what befell its Creator of grave injustice and was troubled and shaken.

The earth was moved, the heavens trembled and the stars became anxious because they could not bear the death of the Son of God, its Maker, in stillness and silence.

There was darkness over all the earth. This could not be attributed to a natural occurrence because a solar eclipse takes place at new moon when the moon is between the sun and the earth. This darkness was a miraculous happening because, at the time of the crucifixion, the Passover of the Jews came at a time when that the moon was opposite the sun as at full moon. This is also evident in the fact that the darkness lasted three hours, from the third hour until the death of Christ at the sixths. Many witnessed this darkness all over the world. St. Dionysius the Areopagite wrote to St. Polycarp that he had experienced this darkness in the city of Heliopolis, in Egypt. Phlegon, a Greek historian wrote, "In the fourth year of the two hundred and second Olympiad, there took place a greater and more extraordinary eclipse than had ever happened before, for at the sixth hour the light of day was changed into the darkness of night, so that the stars appeared in the heavens," St Lucian the martyr also writes, "Look into our annals, and you will find that in the time of Pilate the sun disappeared, and the day was invaded by darkness." All blood that has been shed from the time of creation to that hour could not hold the effectiveness of the blood that was shed upon the cross, for it softened the natural elements to signal the softening of the stony hearts of the gentiles to generate children for Himself despite their cruelty and rebellion.

As one of the fathers said, "In the first creation, before the waters under the firmament were gathered, before the dry land appeared, and before life was bestowed upon all living things, there was darkness all over the earth. This is also true of the new creation before the redemptions of mankind – darkness covered the face of the earth once more."

Here we note:

Firstly - The power of this witness

When the sun shines, the stars disappear, and when the Sun of Righteousness shone upon the cross of wisdom and power, His light reached out to all obscuring even the light of the sun. From that time on, healing was found in His wings extended upon the wood of the cross, and salvation was accomplished and available to all, that none should perish of those that believe in him.

Nature then has announced the divinity of its crucified Creator. Nature resembled blossoming trees in a garden surrounded by a high fence, guarded at night and watered and pruned by day by the Gardener who does not sleep nor slumber. When the thieves attacked and imprisoned the Gardener, the trees thirsted, the leaves dried up and the flowers faded and bowed their heads as a sign of their sadness, and put on sadness in grief over its kind but suffering Master. All creation began to groan and be agitated seeking His return to itself in amazement, "Sustain me with cakes of raisins, Refresh me with apples, For I am lovesick," (Song 2:5).

Children weep for the loss of their father, and servants don mourning garments upon the death of their master. God's Nature also proved, with its lamentation, its deep sorrow for the death of its Creator. The angels weep for their Sustainer and creation for its Creator. Christ died to forgive sins and to deliver creation from the bondage of corruption into the glorious liberty of the children of God (Rom 8:21).

St Jacob of Serug wrote, "He raised His voice in groans and announced that He would entrust His Spirit into the hands of His Father and so creation was moved to weep for the forsaken. The earth trembled, the world shook, the rocks wailed and the stones dissolved. The mountain cried out for help and the hills lamented. The pillars of the universe inclined to collapse upon its inhabitants, but Christ, the Power of the God, upheld them. The earth was moved to escape to nothingness, but He grasped with His might lest it should fall. The Sun hid its light, and the heavens were attired in the colours of great anguish. The daylight took flight and the night entered to become as a veil and a garment for the King whom the crucifiers had stripped naked.

The Sun veiled its eyes that it may not see its Creator exposed. The city of dead heard the voice, its foundations were shaken and it released its dwellers. His voice went up and extinguished all the lights, and went down to Hades and raised all the dead from eternal torment. The veil of the temple was torn in two that all may know that the Chief of all living is dead."

Some ask why God allowed this darkness to come about at the time of Christ's suffering. We answer that through this darkness, the Father has declared His case against mankind, and through nature's manifestation has shamed them. The prophecy of Amos the prophet was fulfilled, "And it shall come to pass in that day, says the Lord God, That I will make the sun go down at noon, And I will darken the earth in broad daylight," (Amos 8:9).

A certain wise man once contemplated that when God appeared on Mount Sinai to bestow the law upon the people of Israel, His presence was in the midst of mist and darkness, (Ex 20:21). The law that prefigured Jesus was introduced at that time. Now, on the Mount of Golgotha, the incarnate Son of God shrouds Himself in a veil of darkness to conceal the anguish of death from the eyes of the wicked in order to accomplish the great work of atonement for the salvation of all. "Behold the Lamb of God who takes away the sin of the world," (Jn 1:29). In the words of another, "With the darkness God laid out His case before heaven and earth against man saying, "Hear, O heavens, and give ear, O earth! For the Lord has spoken: I have nourished and brought up children, And they have rebelled against Me," (Is 1:2). When the heavens witnessed man's sin against his God and Creator its lights were veiled to throw the world into terrible darkness and to alert it to the fact that there it had never before seen such great wickedness.

It has been remarked that the darkness signalled the struggle between Jesus and the spiritual powers of darkness. There is no doubt that this darkness could not compare to the darkness that had gathered over the heart of Christ whilst He bore the burden of all of man's sin.

When the Egyptians tormented Israel, God struck them

with a darkness that lasted for three days as punishment for their wickedness. When the Jews, however, afflicted the Lord of Israel on the cross, the darkness only lasted for three hours. Can you not see that God is abundant in His compassion and generous in His forgiveness? His delight is in our salvation, His labour is for our correction and He is never malevolent.

Do not fear, O Christian, if the injustices of this world engulfs you for it had engulfed your Master before you. All you need to do is follow in His footsteps, "He shall bring forth your righteousness as the light, And your justice as the noonday"

(Ps 37:6).

Our consolation is increased by knowing that the veil of the temple was torn in two from top to bottom," (Matt 27:51). This was evidence that the mystery of redemption has raised the barrier that existed between God and man, and has abolished the discord that was between the Jews and the nations, "For He Himself is our peace, who has made both one, and has broken down the middle wall of separation, having abolished in His flesh the enmity," (Eph 2:14,15).

I thank You, my Lord Jesus, for this great reconciliation, and ask You to raise the barrier of ignorance from me that I may know You in truth.

I am like Isaac who, when he had lost his sight, could not know the true Jacob. This darkness has only deceived me because I am estranged from You. Tear down, O Jesus, the veil of my sins and draw me close to You, "For with You is the fountain of life; In Your light we see light," (Ps 36:9).

Secondly - The significance of this witness

Come Christians to hear the voice of your Saviour saying, "Whilst hanging on the cross, I felt a great distress, not because of My wounds but due to the three hours of darkness for they seemed longer than many years. However, I bore them with contentment and ease, for I was comforted by the light I would reveal to you beyond this darkness."

O that the terror of those hours would raise a strong hatred in souls for sin and reveal to us the great difference between darkness and light, so we may know how to repent and how to bear the fruits of righteousness and holiness.

Nature put on the robe of darkness to cover the nakedness of her Creator. We also can do this. The Lord Christ said, "Let your light so shine before men, that they may see your good works and glorify your Father in heaven," (Matt 5:16). The glory of our Father and the honour of our Redeemer are manifest in our good conduct, for if our conduct is noble we wrap the cross of Christ in the cloak of honour and glory, "By this My Father is glorified, that you bear much fruit; so you will be My disciples," (Jn 15:8). If, however, the odour of our wicked conduct becomes apparent, then it becomes true of us that, "the name of God is blasphemed among the Gentiles because of you," (Rom 2:24). So by our uprightness we become like those elements of nature that had compassion upon its Creator and had covered up His nakedness, but with our wickedness we become like His crucifiers who stripped Him of His garments.

Nature, that had donned the garments of mourning over its Creator, had covered its face in shame and reverence as if to say, "How can I adorn myself while my Master is being treated with contempt," Indeed, you have done well O heavens and earth for you have honoured your Creator and have mourned Him with copious tears. Through the actions of the rocks and tombs, our cruel, faithless and insensitive hearts have been reproached. The solid rocks were tempered by the suffering of its Saviour, but our hearts are not softened instead grow harder every day through the deceitfulness of sin, (Heb 3:13).

Every year all Christian churches commemorate the crucifixion in order to remember the agony and sufferings of the good Lord. As someone once pondered, "People awake from their sleep, start out for their churches. They behold Jesus hanging on the wood of the cross. Some are not affected by this in the least. Others are somewhat affected, but by the evening will have forgotten all about it and will be bowing to those idols dwelling in thier hearts, whether money or beauty or position. How many of this multitude will beat their breasts, horrified before the figure of the crucified One but before darkness could overwhelm them they lay down in the shadows of forgetfulness between the covers of ignorance and apathy."

On this day, scholars stand and contemplate Him who uttered wisdom from upon His cross but the day is not ended before they have returned to their old ignorant philosophies forgetting the cross, "For the message of the cross is foolishness to those who are perishing, but to us who are being saved it is the power of God," (I Cor I:18).

On this day, women busy with the pleasures of life and having a passion for jewellery and finery, go out to see the Mother of Jesus bewailing her only Son at the cross. Once this spectacle is hidden from them, however, they begin to direct their sights to their adornment.

Young people, who flow with the currents of the day without discernment, stand momentarily to see Mary Magdalene washing with her tears the blood off the feet of the crucified One, but as soon as their eyes veer away from this scene they hurry away laughing.

On Great and Holy Friday, our holy church offers an opportunity for ardent worship, ignited by this unique memory, the memory of the sufferings of the Saviour of the world, particularly when the worshippers contemplate the icon of the crucified One on the day when the church becomes the teacher of the truth and divulges to its disciples the lessons of salvation. This it does employing the most sublime teaching methods, by relating the Old Testament symbolism with the truths of the New Testament. It thus pains us to see so many who do not appreciate this work and others who feel it is nothing out of the ordinary and are thus not affected by it.

Therefore, there is none left but you alone, O sun, to show compassion over His trials, and you, O heavens, to lament Him with your tempests, and you, O graves by opening up, and you, O rocks, by cracking open, and you, O wilderness with your quacking, and you, O seas with your roaring. Bewail Him, you His insensible creation for His rational and articulate creation has hardened its heart against Him and has loved sin over Him.

I ask you this, for what day other than this day have you hidden your tears, and for what dead have you saved your weeping? Have you known a righteous benefactor to compare with this abused and slain One? Are you acquainted with a sincere friend akin to Him who was hung naked on the cross? How hard-hearted we are! How is it that we cannot feel or sense His pain nor lament His agony, as if unaware that our transgressions were His crucifiers and our sins His slayers, causing His inanimate creation to bewail Him? Weep bitterly, you Christians, over the suffering of your beloved Saviour!

Let us then with profuse tears cry out saying, "O very sweet Jesus, who was crucified on our behalf, we the sinners who deserve death:

Our hands have plucked the forbidden fruit, but in their stead You have stretched out Yours to be nailed.

Our eyes have looked upon the tree of the knowledge of good and evil, but You O Light of the world, have closed Your eyes on their behalf.

Our ears have listened to the enticement of the serpent, but You have been abandoned to endure words of cursing and blasphemy.

Our mouths have tasted the fruits of transgression, while Yours has tasted bitterness in their stead.

Our feet have walked towards that tree, but, in their stead, Yours have been nailed on to the cross.

Our hearts have lusted and desired, but upon the cross Yours has melted on their behalf.

Every day, my Saviour, I offer my members to be tools for sin, while You offered Yours to be tortured in their stead.

Truly my Lord, marvellous is Your endless and limitless love.

The wise Solomon said, "But if a man lives many years And rejoices in them all, Yet let him remember the days of darkness, For they will be many," (Eccl 11:8). Mediating upon the times of darkness is one of the best means of guidance and direction. Divine providence unleashed the veils of darkness upon the Jewish lands to give an opportunity to the believers, who were at the cross, to meditate on those events, and for the unbelievers to examine their deeds and to repent.

John Chrysostom said, "He who has permitted the heavens to be darkened and to the earth to be shaken, was able to permit the heavens to rain fire and brimstone upon earth and the earth to open and swallow all the treacherous people in retaliation and as punishment for the abasement and death of the Son of God. If it had been His pleasure to shorten His life upon the earth, it was not to diminish His mercy and end His compassion upon us. He thus allowed the elements to be troubled only to warn the transgressor and the guilty without undermining."

St Basil said, "What great mercy God grants man when He touches his hard heart with a crushing ordeal that He may abide within him. Am I not, O righteous Jesus, harder than rocks and more solid than flint stone, for tribulation cannot crush me nor the waters of Your visitation dissolve me. Your voice upon Your death at Golgotha shook the foundations of the earth and shattered the rocks, though You did not die for the sake of the earth or the rocks but for my sake, I who am ailing.

Does not that bitter cry terrify me? May it shatter the crust upon my hard heart and break and dissolve it, for I know that "a broken and a contrite heart, this O God You will not despise."

CHAPTER 10

The Words of Christ Upon the Cross

"The words that I speak to you are spirit, and they are life" (John 6:63)

The last words spoken by those departing from this world are always very dear to their loved ones and have a great significance for they reveal the fruits of the life lived by that person and the product of his experiences.

The words that Christ uttered as He was dying upon the cross had great significance because of the greatness of the utterer and because they were the last words spoken by the friend of mankind after He had won a victory unheard of man's history. Each expression is regarded to have greater importance than a thousand orations for it holds meanings essential for mankind in general. The power of some of the words were not apparent at the time but became clear to succeeding generations.

Now we kneel beside Your cross, O Son of God, so inform us of Your last words and entrust us with Your concluding commandments. Indeed Your suffering did not prevent You from teaching us, so grant that we focus on what You valued and guide us to it.

The words of Christ on the cross are seven in number and this number is a holy and perfect number in the Holy Bible. These also fulfilled prophecies indicated in the Old Testament.

The First Word was prophesied by Isaiah:

Isaiah 53:12

The Second Word also fulfilled Isaiah's words:

Isaiah 53:9-12

The third fulfilled the words spoken by Simeon the Elder:

Lk 2:25

The fourth was literally the words in the Psalm:

Ps 22:1

The fifth, sixth and seventh fulfilled words in the Psalms:
Ps 69:21, Ps 22:31, Ps 31:15

Of these words three were uttered before the earthquake and were full of his grace and blessing. The four spoken after the darkness expounded his service and redemptive work.

The words also indicate that the crucified One is the incarnate God who came to redeem us, and who gave Himself a perfect sacrifice on our behalf to lift our case before the Father and to renew our nature.

THE FIRST WORD

Amazing Pardon

"Then Jesus said, Father, forgive them, for they do not know what they do"
(Lk 23:34)

It was only natural that the first word to be uttered by the Lord upon the cross would be a prayer of forgiveness for those who had treated him with brutal cruelty, for He who had said, "But I say to you, love your enemies, bless those who curse you, do good to those who hate you, and pray for those who spitefully use you and persecute you," (Matt 5:44). He would surely walk in accordance with His own teachings and commandments.

"My Father," - He is declaring to the Father that He is His Son and that He is who is suffering, but that He has forgiven His crucifiers and asks His Father to also forgive them. He excuses them on the basis that they do not know what they are doing. It is as if He is saying, "Lay their offences on Me and do not deem them guilty. Remember that they are Your creation and that You are their Father. Indeed they are wicked, but they are Your children and I have come for their salvation and so have mercy upon them according to Your great mercy."

Christ was demonstrating that there is no barrier between the cross and the throne of God but rather, with confidence He was interceding for His crucifiers. Christ had overlooked His suffering and had asked for their forgiveness. St Paul had said about love that it, "does not seek its own," (I Cor 13:5). Christ did not focus on, nor care about, His pain but, when he saw the pain of the souls of those sinners, He attended to them and asked His Father to forgive their sins. However, He did not dispense with accomplishing His redemptive work. He did not ask Him to bring Him down from the cross nor to deliver Him from the nails nor to lift up from Him the crown of thorns. No, but rather He said, "Free the sinners from the prison of their sins. Though these nails bind Me to the cross, their sins bind them to destruction".

Whenever a man is afflicted with hardship, he no longer cares for anything and the world and all that is in it becomes worthless as compared with his healing. Christ, however, was not concerned about His own suffering but was concerned with the salvation of all sinners. He thus revealed that the destruction of those wretched souls had caused Him greater pain than His torture and suffering. How great is His love!

Saint Augustine said, "He prayed for the sake of those whose cruelty He endured knowing that they did not kill Him but rather that He had willingly died for their sakes." The Jews had demanded of Pilate, "Crucify Him!", but He asks of His Father "Forgive them!" Through this action He sought life for them, while they sought His death. He stretched out His hand to bind their wounds, while His own blood poured forth from the wounds they caused.

It has been said, "He, the greater Being, ascended the altar and stretched out His hands to pray, and while He offered Himself a sacrifice, He defended sinful man."

Who then can measure the enormity of our Saviour's love for us, this love which fills His heart even while still on the cross? The Apostle Paul contemplated, "to know the love of Christ which passes knowledge; that you may be filled with all the fullness of God," (Eph 3:19).

Let us meditate upon Him as He tosses on His fiery bed of suffering, is submerged by waves of grief and the wicked surround Him like locust. While He, long-suffering and patient and in meekness and gentleness, casts loving eyes at those who gloated over Him and who were intoxicated with the wine of victory over Him, and then raises them up to His heavenly Father to ask Him to overlook their great offense.

Every member of His body was wounded except His tongue, which, from the immensity of what had befallen the Lord of pain, bleeding and bitter abuse, was dry like a shard and full of bitterness more than the bitterness of colocynth or wormwood, as in the prophecy, "My strength is dried up like a potsherd, And My tongue clings to My jaws," (Ps 22:15). With this same dry tongue He entreated His Father to forgive those who had caused him such bitter suffering.

The song writer reflects, "love is as strong as death, Jealousy as cruel as the grave; Its flames are flames of fire, A most vehement flame. Many waters cannot quench love, Nor can the floods drown it," (Song 8:6-7).

All the suffering heaped upon the head of the Saviour by those wicked people could not quench the love that burned within His heart for them.

And thus God treats us every day: Though we lift up to Him our evil and offer Him every transgression, He is not only patient with us but blesses us abundantly. The Holy Bible affirms, "For He is kind to the unthankful and evil," (Lk 6:35). If we repent He forgives us our sins and pardons our offenses.

What then does the Saviour desire but to gain victory over us by the power of love not that of vengeance? The death of Christ was, in appearance at least, a defeat, and though He was innocent, could not find anyone to defend Him from those He had benefitted.

So many great people were afflicted in the same way but they were not noble in their affliction. They had uttered bitter words and had died cursing their deliverers and murderers, but Christ was victorious when He said to the Father, "Forgive them."

One of the saintly fathers once said, "For whom did Jesus pray? It was for the Jews who were killing Him who had bestowed upon them His many blessings. He prayed for them in the midst of His violent tortures and severe suffering. Had He prayed for them after His resurrection after His agony had vanished and His sorrows had dissipated , and had tasted the sweetness of the fruits of His death, the matter would not have been so astonishing but rather He was asking for the forgiveness of His enemies whilst they were cursing and abusing Him. He asked forgiveness for His enemies before He had uttered any other expression even about Himself, His mother or John His disciple."

On the Mount of Olives of Gethsemane, He had asked to be delivered from the cup of death but He had conditioned this with His words "if it is possible", but as for His enemies He had asked for their forgiveness without condition or provison. This had caused a certain scholar to comment, "Christ vanquished Satan and hurled him into the depths of hell when He uttered, upon the cross, 'Forgive them'", and another, "You, O Son of God, did not look upon them as an adversary would look upon his enemies, but rather as a father upon his errant children, or as a doctor upon his ailing patient. You are not angry with them but rather You pity them and desire to bring them closer to Your capable Father in order for them to receive healing."

Be sure, all you sinners, that you have forgiveness with the Saviour no matter your sins: forgiveness for your cursing you blasphemers; forgiveness for your false oaths you who swear; forgiveness for your disgrace you who are immoral; forgiveness for your gossiping and malice you wicked.

A pious man once contemplated, "Would that my eye, O my Saviour, was a lamp, my blood oil, my flesh candles, and all that is within and without me melt and burn with Your love."

"For they do not know what they do."

This is a petition for mercy, simple in form, deep in meaning, beautiful in significance. It is the best petition raised to the Father of mercies in heaven. The Saviour understates the offenses of His killers so that the Father may forgive them. The inference of Christ's words then is that those who crucified Him did not realise the greatness of the sin they had committed. This corresponds with the words of the Apostle Peter, "I know that you did it in ignorance, as did also your rulers," (Act 3:17) and those of St Paul, "for had they known, they would not have crucified the Lord of glory," (I Cor 2:8).

We ought to know that Christ did not mention or consider the ignorance of those who killed Him a sufficient excuse to justify them or to gain them forgiveness. Rather He only mentioned it to clarify and declare their condition. Ultimately, ignorance though it lessens the offense and its punishment does not justify the offender. Your lack of appreciation for my person does not entitle you to commit a crime against me, for evil is evil no matter wherever it occurs.

The wise Solomon said, "Do they not go astray who devise evil?" (Prov 14:22). The flesh that is that way inclined will commit evil and its pursuit blinds one's spiritual nature and diminishes one's ability to distinguish good from evil. Sin, then blinds the heart and hardens it, but it is not right that one should use this blindness as an excuse for it emanates from one's freewill and is its companion.

All who commit evil do so in ignorance, for had they known that this evil will be their destruction, they would not have considered doing it. They, however, approach it with self-seeking and sometimes even choose evil under the guise of doing well. He who desires to commit sin closes his mind's eye to its evil and resembles a man who shuts his eyes firmly before throwing himself down from a great height. Regardless of the perpetrator's intentions in committing the sin he will have to bear the consequences.

If the Saviour then forgave His killers, it was not because they were devoid of guilt but rather because of His great love was and to reveal the preciousness of His blood and its efficacy.

As St Basil contemplated, "The mercy of God is affected by two emotions: one that moves it to avenge the sin that offends the holiness of God and His justice; the other invokes His compassion toward us when it sees us caving in under the heavy burdens of sin. In the end the latter overcomes the former."

For whom did the Saviour pray? He prayed for those Roman soldiers who crucified Him in obedience to their leaders, knowing nothing themselves. Perhaps the prayer encompassed the masses who collaborated in His death by consenting to the actions of the authorities, and those who cried out "Crucify Him!" who blindly followed the direction of their leaders, not understanding that Jesus is the Son of God and therefore unaware of the atrocity they were committing.

Secondly, His prayer also included all of mankind including those who preceded His death from Adam and those who followed it to the end of the world, for their sins are the cause of Christ hanging on the cross. You and I are amongst those for whom the

Son of God asked forgiveness. What thanksgiving then should we offer our Saviour, Who cared for the forgiveness of our sins, and is it fitting after all to contradict or oppose His will?

However, did the Chief Priests, who heard His declaration that He is the Son of God and still deliberately rejected Him, benefit from this prayer? This is the sin of blasphemy against the Holy Spirit that is not forgiven in this or the next world. "Anyone who speaks a word against the Son of Man, it will be forgiven him; but whoever speaks against the Holy Spirit, it will not be forgiven him, either in this age or in the age to come," (Matt 12:32). This prayer, then, does not encompass those who know the light and extinguish it so that they can no longer see. Those who, in pride and obstinacy, resist the grace of the Holy Spirit and continue in their callousness and lack of faith will not harvest the fruit of this prayer.

Some ignorance, then, is voluntary and some is involuntary. Jesus prayed for those who are unknowingly ignorant, as St Paul declared, "I was formerly a blasphemer, a persecutor, and an insolent man; but I obtained mercy because I did it ignorantly in unbelief," (I Tim 1:13). The thief on the right and the centurion both of whom witnessed for Christ, were justified, for they were truly ignorant. Caiaphas, on the other hand, chose his ignorance and rejection of Christ, though he knew that He was the Son of God and therefore did not benefit from this petition. To such the Apostle announces, "Therefore you are inexcusable, O man," (Rom 2:1).

We, however, should also learn from this entreaty the necessity of forgiving our enemies who oppress us. For, if God, in all His majestic might, forgave those who injured Him, should we, in our wretchedness and lowly state, not forgive our own adversaries?

Many believe that it is above human nature to forgive their enemies citing the fact that even animals avenge themselves when they are attacked. A sensible person, however, should behave better than an animal and distinguish himself from an animal by being kind to those who abuse him. Those who are unable to overcome their anger and hasten to take revenge as soon as they recall an enemy's offense succumb to a brutal nature. The person who is led by his rational human nature, however, will forgive the offender and moreover will love him and will be compassionate toward him as a physician would love the patient but hate the sickness and do all in his power to eradicate it. Struggle, then, to cure the sickness of your enemy with your love and compassion, "Therefore If your enemy is hungry, feed him; If he is thirsty, give him a drink; For in so doing you will heap coals of fire on his head. Do not be overcome by evil, but overcome evil with good," (Rom 12:20-21). St Peter the Apostle places before us our Saviour as an example of this when he says, "Who committed no sin, Nor was deceit found in His mouth; who, when He was reviled, did not revile in return; when He suffered, He did not threaten, but committed Himself to Him who judges righteously," (I Pt 2:22-23).

Many people fear bearing with the abuse of the wicked lest it be encouraged to continue but as the wise man says, "A soft answer turns away wrath, But a harsh word stirs up anger," (Prov 15:1). The punishment of sin does not affect the perpetrator to the extent as its forgiveness.

If we say that Christ, as the incarnate God, was capable of forgiving His crucifiers but we as humans do not have the same capacity, we should then ponder Joseph as forgives his brothers and David as he rejects harming Saul who seeks to kill him and Stephen as he cries out with a loud voice, "Lord, do not charge them with this sin," (Acts 7:59,60) as he is being stoned to death and St Paul as he says, "Being reviled, we bless; being persecuted, we endure," (I Cor 4:12). We might also consider St Cyprian who, when condemned to die by the sword, ordered twenty-five pieces of gold to be given the executioner who administered the sentence with trembling hand. Nothing affects the soul as much as the forgiveness of wrongdoing.

There is no doubt that the Lord's forgiveness had a more profound effect on the souls than revenge ever could have had and this incident is still a fragrant scent that spreads to attract many.

It is said that a missionary once related to a native chief the story of Christ's forgiveness upon the cross. Once he had finished, the chief commanded him to leave the country explaining that were the missionary to be allowed to speak these words to the people he feared they would be attracted to Christianity for no such teaching existed in the religion of the land.

St Paul advised, "do not let the sun go down on your wrath," (Eph 4:26-27). So many people go to sleep with hostility entrenched in their hearts. What would they do if death comes suddenly upon them while they still bore enmity toward others? Are they then able to approach the gate of heaven offering God their enmity?

The Second Word

Amazing Forgiveness

"Assuredly, I say to you, today you will be with Me in Paradise" (Lk 23:43)

Christ between two thieves - the Innocent between two thieves. Why was this so? He had said to them, at the time of His arrest, "Have you come out, as against a thief, with swords and clubs to take Me?" (Matt 26:55). They thought that He resented being treated as a thief. They preferred Barabbas the insurrectionary over Him and crucified Jesus between two thieves.

There is, however, no situation in this world that may not be used for the glory of God no matter its causes or reasons. St Jacob of Serug said, "The Judge chose to demonstrate the verdict upon Golgotha and so He set the sheep on His right hand and the goats on the left." They put Him among sinners but He showed us that He accepts sinners even at the time of their deaths. He was between the two thieves as a Shepherd in the midst of stray sheep and a physician attending His sick. They drew Him in to die and He gave life to the dead. They took Him into the house of judgement and He vindicated the sinful. They gave Him the cup of suffering to drink and He bound their wounds and healed them.

Let us now meditate what emerges from the right hand thief and the Saviour's response. The thief showed perfect faith and the Saviour complete forgiveness. Afflictions occur to people as a consequence of their sins. Some benefit from these afflictions while others do not. The two thieves were condemned to death by crucifixion - the thief on the right felt that he deserved the punishments as opposed to the thief on the left who began to taunt Christ. His associate rebuked him saying, "Do you not even fear God, seeing you are under the same condemnation?" (Lk 23:40).

What was it that affected the emotions of this thief and made him reveal such tender feelings? No doubt the serenity of the Saviour's condition touched his heart, changed his disposition and enlightened his mind. No doubt also hearing Him utter the words, "Father, forgive them," had the greater part to play in drawing his heart closer to this crucified One Whose heart is empty of all hatred toward His enemies. He must have believed that He who forgives His killers could not possibly have committed any offence warranting death and so he said to the other thief, "And we indeed justly, for we receive the due reward of our deeds; but this Man has done nothing wrong," (Lk 23:41).

A person who senses his sins also senses his need for a Saviour. The right thief's feeling of culpability led him to ask of Jesus, "Lord, remember me when You come into Your kingdom," (Lk 23:42). It is remarkable that: Peter denies his Master before a servant girl, while the thief declares his faith openly; the two disciples on the way to Emmaus say "but we had hoped that he was the one," while the thief says with firm hope "Remember me"; Thomas cries out saying, "Unless I see in His hands the print of the nails, and put my finger into the print of the nails, and put my hand into His side, I will not believe," while the thief confesses Him to be a King while still on the cross!

St Augustine contemplated, "Where can there be anything evil with Him, and without Him where can there be anything good?" and another said, "Glorifying God, I say that through His actions and faith, this thief has put to shame all those who stood around the cross of Christ. Moreover, he has reproached and shamed the Apostles also for the weakness of their faith and their troubled hearts. He still puts to shame all who reject faith in Christ, who even now sits at the right hand of the Father in heaven for he believed in Him while He was hanging on the cross in the depth of humility and shame."

God had revealed to the thief the truth, and he had used this to his benefit. God reveals to many the reality of their condition but they are not convinced, and consequently do not draw near to ask for forgiveness. The thief, however, hastened to seize the opportunity before he missed it and asked for mercy in its time. For this reason he deserved to hear the Voice saying, "today you will be with Me in Paradise."

Christ's enemies had gloated over Him and His beloved ones had despaired of His salvation, but the thief alone had defended the Saviour against his fellow-thief. Accordingly God had given him the light, and by that light he had known the way of salvation and had immediately walked in it saying to the Lord, "Remember me".

The thief had offered the Saviour an astonishing supplication confessing that he was a sinner and that the Saviour was the Forgiver. In brokenness, he had entreated Him in the midst of all the gloating of the enemy and the sadness of the loved ones. Indeed, the thief alone was able to see the glory of the Redeemer in the midst of the darkness that had engulfed the cross.

At all times, God does not leave Himself without a witness, even on the cross. The thief was the only one witness of Christ's divinity. The Lord had found many, after His resurrection, to call Him Lord, but on the cross He found no one to call Him Lord apart from the thief. We understand by this that the wicked are not bereft of goodness but this needs strength to be revealed, and there is no strength that is able to reveal goodness in the wicked as that of meditating upon the suffering of Christ.

The Bible informs us that, in the beginning, both thieves

blasphemed the Lord, but the suffering of Christ and His patience caused the thief on the right to cease his blasphemy. Then he used the same mouth that had formerly blasphemed to confess the divinity of the One crucified with him, and did not doubt that His kingdom began after His death as He had said, "Therefore My Father loves Me, because I lay down My life that I may take it again," (Jn 10:17).

Who then had informed the thief of these unfathomable mysteries so that he discerned that He who is crucified with him is God and that His kingdom is eternal, though He was suffering pain, was naked and though His body was bleeding profusely? The Jews had scorned Him supposing that they had been victorious over Him depriving Him of His temporal kingdom. No doubt that these mysteries had been revealed to Him by the Spirit of truth. Yes, the thief had called Christ his Lord though He was crucified like him, and in his confession there was:

Faith, Hope, Love and Humility

For he did not say to Him, "If You are able, remember me," but he said with perfect faith "Remember me," as if to say, "All things are possible to You," He did not say, "If You will, remember me," for he doubted not His love. He did not ask to be taken with Him, but in humility was satisfied to just be remembered by Him, as if to say, "O Lord of infinite mercy do not forget me when You come into Your kingdom. Where will my numerous sins lead me? It is sufficient for me to be able to glimpse Your glory, and to find a place in Your heart. Then I will not be forgotten by You, and I will not ask for pardon nor love for I am a sinner, but will only ask to be remembered by You."

One of the church fathers contemplated, "Who taught you, O thief, this adoration to such a scorned and rejected man who hangs with you on the wood of a tree? Indeed, the eternal Light, who enlightens all those who dwell in darkness and the shadow of death, has taught you. He has condemned Adam your father to death, but you He has given a verdict of pardon and life," St Gregory also writes, "On the cross nails had fastened his hands and feet, and nothing remained free from torture, but his heart and tongue. By the inspiration of God, the thief offered to Him the whole which he found free, that as it is written, With the heart he might believe to righteousness, with the mouth he might confess to salvation. But the three virtues which the Apostle speaks of, the thief suddenly filled with grace both received and preserved on the cross. He had faith, for example, who believed that God would reign whom he saw dying equally with himself. He had hope who asked for an entrance into His kingdom. He preserved charity also zealously in his death, who for his iniquity reproved his brother and fellow-thief, dying for a like clime to his own."

The thief, therefore, was saved not only because he had confessed, but also because he had believed and loved. God will, also, not forgive us our sins merely because we confess them but we will attain forgiveness if we believe that He is capable of forgiveness, and if we love Him in the full knowledge that this forgiveness results from His love for us.

This is what was manifested from the thief. Let us now turn to what transpired from the Saviour - Perfect Mercy.

The thief had asked Him to remember him in His Kingdom on the last day, but the Saviour had answered him "today". He did not say, "After years or months or even days of contemplating your sins I will take you to Paradise," but rather "today," that is "before the setting of the sun you will be carried from the cross to Paradise," How great is Christ's generosity and abundant His compassion? In His first expression on the cross "forgive them," He has shown that He is the Priest who mediates on behalf of the guilty, and in His second that He is the King who is prepared to accept the penitent to Himself in His Kingdom.

The Saviour was not willing to respond to His abusers and cursers, but He would not be silent in accepting the thief and in telling him that he would carry him from the house of tribulation to the house of eternity, and from the adversity of the cross to the bliss of paradise. Those who serve the world will not acquire from it a reward anywhere equal to their efforts. The thief spent his life serving the world and his only recompense was the cross. When however, the thief truly loved Christ even though for a brief period, he received an inconceivable reward. He is thus amongst those of the eleventh hour, and to him applies the Lord's response to him of the first hour, "I wish to give to this last man the same as to you. Is it not lawful for me to do what I wish with my own things?" (Matt 20:14-15).

Jesus gives more than we can imagine and even more than we deserve. Hear Him as He says to Peter, "Where I am going you cannot follow Me now, but you shall follow Me afterward," (Jn 13:36). But He says to the thief, "Today you will be with Me." Today you are with Me in sorrow, but on that same day you will also be with Me in joyfulness. Adam was snatched from Paradise by Satan and was delivered to Hades, but the Saviour snatched man whilst at the gate to Hades and returned him to Paradise.

Dearly beloved do you see this thief hanging on the cross beside Christ? Do you see the copious sweat pouring down his brow and his pale face? Do you see the silent grief overcoming him? Do you

witness the phantoms of death that hover over his head? Do you
observe the demons of Hades gathering around his feet waiting
to devour him as if he were a palatable morsel? Examine his chest
to find the words, "Doomed," and "Condemned," written over it.
Consider his heart to see the darkness of Hades and its blackness
gathered within it. This thief, with one foot in the grave, utters
this notable prayer, "Lord, remember me when You come into
Your kingdom,"

Now go back and look at him again. Where is the sweat on
his brow and the paleness of his face? Where is the silent grief?
It has all dispersed like a summer cloud and has been replaced by
an angelic smile. Where are demons of Hades? They have fled
and scattered and in their place the Seraphim with white radiant
wings waiting to snatch his soul that has become a matchless pearl
to decorate the crown of the Lord of glory. Where now is the
word "condemned," that was written over his chest? It has been
wiped away and replaced with the word "Justified". Where is the
darkness and blackness that had once filled his heart? They have
dispersed and his heart has become as luminous as the sun! Cast
another look toward the triumphant - who is this sitting in their
midst, more luminous than the sun and more dazzling than the
moon? This is the thief. How swift a change: In the morning
driven as a criminal and in the evening justified and saved from
his sins; In the morning condemned to death as if not deserving
to live among people, and in the evening accepted and welcome as
if family, living among the citizens of heaven.

St Augustine said that the word "Amen," or "assuredly,"
was used by Christ as a kind of pledge so that the thief may be
reassured, (for the reward promised him was extremely great), so
that it was not too difficult for him, (considering his condition),

to believe that he would receive this great glory or to believe that Christ, while still crucified, could grant this excellent gift. The Jews also had imagined Paradise to be an abode for the body not the soul, and so the Saviour reassured him.

If the thief rejoiced because he was saved, Christ was even more delighted for He saw the efficacy of His blood and its ability to purify the wickedest of sinners, and that His cross had became a royal throne for justice and power. He reigned from it as the King of mercy and forgave the sinner, to demonstrate to the world that His death upon the cross is salvation to the damned.

The Paradise that the Saviour referred to is the place in which rests the souls of the believers after their deaths till the Day of Resurrection, when they will be in the presence of Christ enjoying the fruits of the Tree of Life, as Adam and Eve did when they were in Paradise. The purpose, then, of Paradise is to grant bliss to the souls of the righteous as a pledge for the glory of the life that eye has not seen, nor ear heard, nor has entered into the heart of man.

The Saviour had said to the thief, "today you will be with Me in Paradise," and not "today you will be with Me in My kingdom," for the kingdom is the place of contentment for both the body and the soul, and this kingdom will not come until the Day of Judgement when we will rise in our glorified bodies. Christ then was addressing the spirit of the thief.

From the above then we can note the following:

I. The breadth of the mercies of God toward those who serve Him faithfully and diligently, for His suffering did not divert His attention away from the thief who was pleading for his salvation. In His heavenly abode He listens to the penitent and grants forgiveness. He is silent when He considers the thousands who blaspheme His blessed name. Jesus cares for our salvation more than we do ourselves and that is why He died that we may live forever.

2. The cross which was deemed in the sight of people a spectacle of weakness, was in fact proof of majesty and power, for with it the host of the enemy was defeated, and before it the sting of death was broken and the dominion of hell was abolished.

3. We learn from the destruction of the thief on the left that the cause of the destruction of man is the ruthlessness of his heart. Had he been accepted why then was forgiveness granted to one and not the other. We answer - it is because the latter placed his sins as a barrier between himself and grace. From this we can understand that the grace of God is not achieved without mankind's freewill. Salvation, though granted freely from God, depends upon both man's will and God's grace. The tenderness of the heart of Christ in His forgiveness of His slaughterers did not affect the thief on the left, nor did his punishment soften him nor the rebuke of the repentant fellow-criminal, the piercing darkness or the earthquake, though his associate had repented before all these happenings. God's grace was sufficient for the salvation of both thieves, but the cause of the destruction of one came from within, as the salvation of the other came through the grace of God working with his freewill.

The angelic vocation itself did not prevent the fall of some of the angels. Similarly the apostolic vocation did not keep Judas from destruction. God's great mercy, then, does not guarantee salvation to the free soul if this mercy is not utilised to attain this salvation.

4. It is easy for some to delay their repentance to the moment of their death, but St Paul urges, "Today, if you will hear His voice, Do not harden your hearts as in the rebellion," (Heb 3:15). Those who await death to repent have the most dangerous example of the thief on the left, for he would not soften toward Jesus though He was his partner in his pain. How many souls expected salvation at death only to realise that their hearts were more callous than they were at any other time, and so departed whilst blaspheming, cursing and growling.

The thief on the left perished because he did not consider the salvation of his soul as did the other, but rather he thought about the salvation of his body, "If You are the Christ, save Yourself and us." At the time of death, many sinners become attentive to their physical rather than their spiritual healing and die in their sins. The thief on the left attributed his suffering to Christ's inability to save him and did not remember his wickedness which was the cause of his death. Many, when they are punished for their sins, do not recall them in order to show remorse but rather grumble against the Lord because He punished them and did not allow them to pursue the path they love. He who postpones his repentance to the time of his death is a fool for if it happens that some attain the grace of remorse in their last days, not all will.

Let us then cry out from this moment, "Lord, remember me."

5. God's promise of the acceptance of sinners encompasses even the wickedest of men. What a most pleasing and joyful promise it is for those whose hearts have been filled with despair due to their deadly sins. The action of the blood of Christ is more powerful than that of your sins, and His righteousness is able to cover your sins. So depend on Him with all your heart

and lean your head upon His cross and be sure that He died for you. Then, O sinner, a spring of comfort that does not dry out will flow for you, and you will experience from Jesus an amazing compassion for the penitent that you have never dreamed of before.

THE THIRD WORD

Amazing Care

"Woman, behold your son! … "Behold your mother!" (Jn 19:26-27)

"A sword will pierce through your own soul – also that the thoughts of many hearts may be revealed." (Lk 2: 35)

The Virgin's Agony

Before we contemplate the Saviour's third word, we will think upon the agony of His distraught mother while she watches Him suffering as a fulfilment of the prophecy of Simeon the Elder, "A sword will pierce through your own soul."

When the Virgin St Mary had heard this prophecy and had known that her Son is the Saviour of the world, she was certain of the advent of this hour in which He would be lifted up onto the cross. How great then was her anguish and how grievous was her pain! When a mother sees that her son is sick, she melts under the grief of not knowing whether the sickness will end in death or healing. The Virgin, however, watched her Son all His life as if watching someone who is ill and being certain of His crucifixion and death and so was accompanied by deep sadness whenever she recalled this. As someone once contemplated, "Our Holy Lady the Virgin nursed her Son and from the drops of this virgin milk that trickled from His mouth, she perceived the drops of blood that would pour forth from His body on the day of His crucifixion, as if to say, 'This milk that my Son sucks now will become blood that will be shed.'" This agrees with the sentiments of the beloved in the Song, "A bundle of Myrrh is my beloved to me that lies all night between my breasts," (Song 1:13).

Indeed, as Abraham journeyed three days up a mountain expecting to slaughter his son, his sadness over Isaac must have been great. The anguish the Virgin must have experienced lasted thirty years. Contemplate then, you righteous souls, the life of the blessed Virgin whose suffering was incessant. Imagine how our lives would be considered happy if they would be spent in contemplating the suffering of our Saviour, so that we may finally attain the exultation the Virgin attained after enduring this exceedingly great pain.

Let us contemplate the occurrences to know the sharpness of the sword that pierced through the soul of the mother of the Saviour. No doubt that, on the eve of His crucifixion, she knew what was about to happen to Him, so what was her condition on that night? As one pious father once reflected, "How did you spend that great night, the eve of the passion and death your Beloved while the rest slept or absorbed in pleasure and amusement? No doubt you kept vigil till morning and as Jeremiah said, 'She weeps bitterly in the night her tears are on her cheeks," (Lam 1:2)'".

John the beloved came to the mother of his Teacher in the morning and told her that her Son was at that moment carrying His cross and going up to the Golgotha, and asked her to rise to bid Him farewell. While awaiting His passing along the way she heard the disturbance of the soldiers and saw the implements of torture they were carrying before Him and then saw Him exhausted and bearing His heavy cross and the blood flowing from His wounds. She scrutinized His body and saw that the scourging had torn His flesh and her heart was broken. His body bled and her eyes poured forth tears as the flow of a river. She lifted her eyes to His head to find it crowned with sharp thorns, His face covered in blood and she herself felt her brow pierced by the same and she wept bitter tears.

Had she enough strength left to stand and see her Son as He passed her? Had she enough ability left to implore His crucifiers for mercy or to open her mouth to say her last farewell to her Son. She had no breath, heart or energy but after much effort she barely mustered the strength to address her Son.

Who is able to express to us the extent of a mother's yearning, at that moment, to be near her Son and to talk to Him? She lingered till He came past and then her eyes met His. Who would not melt in grief at this moving scene? The mother accompanied her Son to Golgotha and there watched as they stripped Him and stretched Him out on the cross. She saw and heard them hammer nails into His hands and feet.

They lifted Him up on the cross and she would not depart from the place so she could witness the death of her Son. She approached the cross, John by her side, and so was able to hear her Son' directive. St John himself testifies, "Now there stood by the cross of Jesus His mother, ..." (Jn 19:25).

It is customary that if one is condemned to death they refuse the presence of their relatives and friends, especially at the time of the execution, so as not to add to their suffering. Christ, however, suffered not only His own intense physical pain but also the anguish of seeing His beloved suffering along with Him.

Eve looked upon the tree in Paradise with all longing till she brought upon us misery, but St Mary would not turn her gaze away from the tree of life which brought forth for us salvation and happiness.

Meditate O my soul then on the extent of the great patience of this mother who suffered this pain to teach us to endure, rather than flee tribulation and suffering for the sake of Christ. The imprudent are those who evade adversity and flee hardship. Take for yourself, O my soul, the example of your great teacher

Jesus Christ, who lived His life on earth experiencing all kinds of human suffering. You are to follow Him and take the same path, and to take His mother as an example of patience in suffering. Though she knew well of His innocence, she did not grumble or complain or bewail her Son as other mothers do. She preferred the glory of God and the salvation of man over the deliverance of her Son, emulating Jesus who also desired the same over His physical deliverance.

The Son's Counsel to His Mother

The Lord saw His mother suffering and John beside her and so He said, "Woman, behold your son!" and to the disciple, "Behold your mother". He did not call her Mother but Woman so as not to add to her agony.

It is a lovely lesson to know that the Saviour looked down from the cross to see many who had congregated around Him, among them the rich, the important, the powerful, the leaders and the priests but the Lord turned His sight away from them and toward a small group of poor women to teach us worldly appearances do not matter to Him. Many people are venerated and exalted by the world but are despised by God, and how many others are ignored and overlooked by people but have a central place in the heart of God.

As one of the saints observed, "What did you go out to see? A prophet? But greater than a prophet. A king? Yes and greater than a king. His throne was the cross of scorn and His crown was of twisted thorns. Come to see the majesty of God. Men despise the cross so the Son of God chose it as His throne. People trample upon the poor and needy but the Son of God welcomes them. Society discards the sinful woman as if she were a wilting or decaying flower, but the Son of God accepts her return and forgives her sins.

It is a great distinction for St John to be in such a position of trust. Truly he was worthy of it for he showed more compassion toward his Master than others, and though he followed from afar, he never left nor forsook the cross. He was thus worthy to become a son to the Virgin. What could be more sublime the home that was occupied by St Mary and St John? If there could be found a house that resembled heaven, in which angels speak of spiritual matters, it would have been this one. History tells us that John remained in Jerusalem and did not leave Palestine until the departure of the soul of the Virgin.

We learn the following from the words of Christ:

I- The excellence of the benefit of sitting at the foot of the cross. We merit this if we live a life of faith and godliness, for he who lives tarnished by guilt and heedless of repentance is unqualified to stand before the cross of Christ, which is the ladder of salvation. Standing before the cross indicates a feeling of the need for the help of the crucified One. Those who have regretted their sins and have crucified the body along with their passions and desires, derive from their presence before the cross, strength to resist the devil who will flee from them (Js 4:7) because at the cross they see the son of God victorious over the powers of evil.

Also those who have lived the life of faith are in need of continually standing before the cross, for Christ did not leave the cross until He had defeated every enemy. As a certain believer once commented, "As the angels constantly ascended and descended the ladder of Jacob, so too those who wish to traverse the path of virtue must follow the cross without ceasing or delaying."

2- Nothing will divert the Lord's sight away from us. While He was suffering upon the cross, He cared for His mother the Virgin. In this there is great comfort for us, for even with the loftiness of His glory and the greatness of His eminence, He commiserates with us and shares our pain. He identifies Himself as our Brother and the Son of God. Now because He sits at the right hand of His Father, He looks at us to comfort us as the best brother and most faithful friend.

3- God permits trials but along with them, He provides the way out. St Joseph, the Virgin's betrothed had died and now her Son also was dying. For this reason He commits her to the care of John the Beloved. God does not permit that something is taken away from us without restitution. He does not bear to wound us with one hand unless He binds the wound with the other.

4- Christ imparts an important lesson to children regarding their duties toward their parents. The Lord fulfilled His responsibilities toward His mother at the most perilous time for Him. However, we see many who believe that they are absolved of their responsibilities towards their parents, loved ones and friends during difficult times.

THE FOURTH WORD

Amazing Abandonment

"My God, My God, why have You forsaken Me?"

(Matt 27:46)

Many wonder why the Son of God cried out saying "My God," and not "My Father".

Yes, as He was not born and baptised nor did He hunger and thirst for His own sake but for ours, so too His cry to the Father, "My God, My God," was for our sake and on our behalf, for He had taken Adam's flesh and had come to pay his debt. For his sake and on his behalf and that of his offspring, He called and cried out. He was in every way just as we are, yet without sin. He came, hungered, thirsted, was wearied and slept. He asked about the quantity of bread they had and where they had laid Lazarus, as One who is ignorant of things though He knows everything even before it exists.

His cry did not emerge from a desire to grumble or complain of injustice; rather it was a cry of someone who has placed His heart in the hands of the Father whom He has obeyed. It was a cry of great distress for what He endured in obeying the Father. He was expressing to His Father the extent of what He had suffered in the way of fulfilling the will of the Father revealing to the world His grace. The Saviour was not trying to be relieved from the work but rather showing His resoluteness in finishing it no matter the cost.

The Saviour said "My God, why have You forsaken Me?" by way of astonishment and amazement not for scrutiny and explanation. Just as the enquiry regarding the healing of the woman with a flow of blood was to declare her faith, so the question here "why have You forsaken Me?" was not due to His lack of insight into the reason, but so the hearers can explore the reason and know that He represented Adam and his offspring. For, if men are abandoned by God, they cannot cross-examine Him with a "Why?" for they are guilty. Christ, however, uttered "Why?" that we may know that He was abandoned, not for misdeeds He committed, but for our own. Then if we know His position as our representative, we can then easily understand why He referred to the Father as "My God". Certainly humanity that had been unable to lift its face up to the Father in jubilation crying out "My God ...My God," for it has been reconciled through the blood of this righteous crucified One. As for the saying, "Why have You forsaken Me", it does not mean that the Father had abandoned Him but rather that the trial was severe and that the Father did not intervene to reduce the suffering or make it superficial.

One interpreter believed that Christ's cry after the darken-ss and earthquake was to reveal that He was alive for the duration of the three hours of darkness and that He was the source of the marvel. The reason He cried out then was not that His divinity had left Him, but that all may see the immensity of what had been done to Him. It was also to show His humanity (for the signs that had been performed had raised doubts in this) and to teach us to resort to the living God in times of tribulation.

The reason for this expression was not the suffering caused by man, for the sinful hands that had held and nailed Him to the cross could not obstruct the brilliance of His Father's face from Him. He cried out because of what the Father had turned His face from. The wrath of man can be endured but the wrath of God is unbearable. Who could imagine the suffering of our blessed Redeemer when Justice raised its sword for recompense from the person of the Representative? "Deep calls unto deep at the noise of Your waterfalls; All Your waves and billows have gone over me," (Ps 42:7). If the waves of human injustice were thrashing Him, they would have been as the waves upon the sea, for underneath them our Redeemer was allotted the depth of immeasurable suffering to which He had to plummet in order to reach us who were slumbering in our grave sins, to raise us from there, and to place us before God in complete and endless contentment.

Consider O my soul, for this intense cry has ushered in the atonement and the descent of fire upon the altar that the Lamb, on which our sins have been placed, may be consumed. The Son has carried on your behalf that which you were unable to carry for yourself. He has done all for us and has left nothing for us but to have faith in Him, to obey His commandments and to have confidence in the sufficiency of His blood for our salvation.

Truly, what could be more remarkable and how great is the sacrifice of the Son of God in accepting this intercessory role before divine justice. He Who gives rest to all who are heavy-laden, is moved with great sadness. He Who wipes the tears of the sad, seeks consolation.

Your entreaty to Your Father is my entreaty that You offer on my behalf. Your pain and weakness upon the cross are recovery and healing for me who is ailing. The punishment that fell due to You has atoned for my sins. Indeed, You sank into the depths of sorrow to establish for me eternal joy.

Why did You cry out My Saviour? You are our Liberator from eternal darkness, but we see You walking in darkness without light. Darkness came and Your suffering was intensified. Darkness without pain is wearisome, and night for the ailing is more difficult than the day. So Your suffering was at its greatest when the darkness came over the earth. You endured all this to transfer us sinners from darkness to Your wonderful light (I Pet 2:9).

Reflect on the fact that Christ was abandoned to His suffering for quite some time without comfort. He was not left between His fiends but between His enemies. When previously His soul had been troubled, a voice came from heaven to encourage Him, (Jn 12:27-28). When He was troubled in Gethsemane, an angel appeared to Him to strengthen Him. Now, however, He crosses the valley of the shadow of death alone. Though God shines His sun upon the righteous and the wicked, and causes rain to fall upon the good and the oppressive, but when His Son became a sin sacrifice, the sun hid its light and the earth withheld even a drop of water from Him.

Jesus bearing the tribulation of the cross teaches us a striking lesson in patience in affliction. Lord, we cannot know how much You endured upon the cross. Help us to take You as an example so that we may not despair if the doors of reprieve close before us and so that we may have comfort in the face of adversity.

This bitter cry was meant to guide us in many matters:

I. With this cry, the Son has restored to humanity what it had lost. The Saviour said, "The kingdom of heaven is like a merchant seeking beautiful pearls, who when he had found one pearl of great price went and sold all that he had and bought it," (Matt 13:45,46). The Father was gratified with the Son as One who is most cherished, "The Father Himself who sent Me has testified of Me," (Jn 5:36). He bought us rest with His labour and joy with His sorrow. Praise to our Saviour who restored all we had lost for it was not in anyone else's capacity except the Son of God.

2. We learn that this abandonment was one of the severest of all of Christ's suffering. I thank You Jesus for this great sacrifice. Your Father turned His face for a short period so that He may not abandon us forever.

Though Christ saw that the Father had abandoned Him, He trusted Him. In truth the Father did not leave Jesus, for at that very moment Jesus was doing the work that God was pleased to allot Him in which He was guarantor of sinners and their mediator.

Do you not then fear sin, you who love it? Do you now know how much God detests it? Could you bear that He could turn His face from you for eternity? Moses had said to the Lord, "If Your Presence does not go with us, do not bring us up from here," (Ex 33:15). How then can you proceed through life and the face of God not before you because you bear sin?

3. Through this cry we learn the virtue of humility. Some have said that it is a virtue only associated with Christ for it was never mentioned in the books of the philosophers and it shines in all works He accomplished in His life. If He was not humble it would not have been said of Him, "Who, being in the form of God, did not consider it robbery to be equal with God, but made Himself of no reputation, taking the form of a bondservant, and coming in the likeness of men," (Phil 2: 6-8). St John said of

Him, "We beheld His glory, the glory as of the only begotten of the Father," (Jn 1:14), but He came down from His position of glory when He gave Himself up for the cross. He was mighty but hid His might so that He was struck by the most base of men. He was wise, but His wisdom was concealed at the cross for He did not utter a word in response. He was great in His kingdom, but this eminence was hidden when He reached the depth of His affliction.

He would also reveal to us, from behind the veil of humility, another teaching and that is, "God … gives grace to the humble," (1Pet 5:5), and so St Paul said of Him, "Therefore God also has highly exalted Him and given Him the name which is above every name, that at the name of Jesus every knee should bow, of those in heaven, and of those on earth, and of those under the earth, and that every tongue should confess that Jesus Christ is Lord, to the glory of God the Father," (Phil 2: 9-11).

He, then, who desires to acquire true greatness must imitate his good Saviour and take the path of humility so that this saying may apply to him, "Let the lowly brother glory in his exaltation," (Js 1:9).

THE FIFTH WORD

Amazing Need

"I thirst!" (Jn 19:28)

One of the consequences of crucifixion was that the crucified were afflicted with an unquenchable thirst, particularly if they are subjected to the burning heat of the sun. When the Saviour felt an intense thirst He cried out "I thirst!"

An amazing need and a strange matter that bewilders the mind! Does He Whom the wind and the seas obey, Who "binds up the water in His thick clouds," (Job 26:8), "Who has measured the waters in the hollow of His hand," (Is 40:12), "and sends waters on the fields", cry out "I thirst". Is the rich man in want and does he who is generous ask for charity? Does the Lord of creation ask for something so trivial, which the poorest of men may acquire effortlessly. What profound sadness? Does the beloved Son thirst? He who turned water to wine in the wedding in Cana of Galilee is in need of water! He who brought forth water from a rock in the wilderness says "I thirst". You women, who stand at the cross, if this appeal does not affect the hearts of His cruel crucifiers, does it not affect you? His torturers have withheld water from Him and now offer Him distasteful sour wine mixed with gall instead. Not from compassion or to quench His thirst, but rather to inflict greater suffering.

The Saviour had felt thirsty from the beginning of His crucifixion. This thirst was made even more severe by the flood flowing profusely from all His wounds. Despite this He patiently endured the thirst for three hours not revealing it until just before His death. Soldiers wounded on the battlefield ask for water before anything, but the Saviour left it till last.

Though Christ did thirst, there was another underlying motive for His words. When He spoke to the Samaritan woman He opened with the words "Give Me a drink," (Jn 4:7). He was not, then, in need of water to quench His thirst, but rather wanted to bring her to the living water as shown by His saying, ""If you knew the gift of God, and who it is who says to you, 'Give Me a drink,' you would have asked Him, and He would have given you living water," (Jn 4:10). How can He thirst who said, "If anyone thirsts, let him come to Me and drink," (Jn 7:37). He is the one who said of Israel, "They have forsaken Me, the fountain of living waters, And hewn themselves cisterns—broken cisterns that can hold no water," (Jer 2:13).

They offered the Saviour sour wine at the time of His thirst, but He did not suffer as much from its bitter taste as from the cruelty of the hearts of those who offered it. He suffered more from the clinging to sin than from the bitter drink. Job said about the sinner, "The food in his stomach turns sour," (Job 20:14), and St Peter said to Simon the sorcerer, "For I see that you are poisoned by bitterness and bound by iniquity," (Act 8:23). St Paul also said of the unrighteous, "Whose mouth is full of cursing and bitterness," (Rom 3:14).

How lamentable! At a time when God is saving mankind, they are censuring Him. He seeks their rescue, and they participate in His torture. How many are they, in each generation, who enjoy the life and blessings God has given them, yet lift up the bitterness of their transgressions and the sourness of their wickedness to Him. What great callousness! God shows such ardour in the matter of our salvation, while we show such disregard for our own souls. The Son of God is crucified, is tortured, thirsts and suffers but desires to save us from sin that leads us to eternal damnation, while we disdain His crucifixion, belittle His suffering, scorn His thirst and do not heed His affliction. At the same time we degrade our own souls, for this rebellion can only lead to our injury and even destruction. If you consider your soul is worthless to you, know that it is precious, for Christ thirsted and died for it.

How many people grieve upon hearing the words of Christ, "I thirst," and desire to have been present to offer Him the finest drink in the most precious vessel, but at the same time contribute to His thirst through their vile deeds? Then, on the cross, He thirsted for water but now upon His throne of Glory He thirsts for the salvation of sinners. Those who sin offer Him a drink much more bitter than was offered Him upon the cross. As He said then of them, "For my thirst they gave me vinegar to drink," (Ps 69:21), so He says now of us, "Why then, when I expected it to bring forth good grapes, did it bring forth wild grapes?" (Isa 5:4), as if to say, "From those, for whose salvation I laboured and for whom I endured the bitterness of thirst, I asked to quench My thirst by leaving their wicked deeds and by walking in faith and love. Instead they have provided bitter fruit - wickedness, corruption and the love of the world - and have added to My suffering and reminded Me of My thirst upon the cross.

If you then wish to comfort your Saviour, quench His thirst and diminish His suffering, offer Him your genuine repentance and your ardent remorse. Christ said, "A woman, when she is in labour, has sorrow because her hour has come, but as soon as she has given birth to the child, she no longer remembers the anguish, for joy that a human being has been born into the world," (Jn 16:21). Christ suffered for our sins upon the cross and from the intensity of its punishment He thirsted but the return of even one sinner to Him will quench this thirst.

His crucifiers would not offer Him water to quench his thirst right up to the moment of His death. Do we also wish to live and die in our sins, leaving the Saviour in His thirst through our lack of repentance? We should fear that to some of us Jesus may say, "I'm going away, and you will seek me and you will die in your sin," (Jn 8:21).

Christ now says, "I thirst and this will quench Me: the elders guiding My church in wisdom; young men seeking My will and working diligently, mothers affectionately raising My children; young women living in My holiness; the strong helping My brethren the poor and the shepherds vigilantly caring for My flock. I thirst for all virtue and he who attains them quenches My thirst and satisfies My hunger."

Let us now ponder this sweet and kind voice, and think well upon what we shall do. Shall we listen and obey, or linger in our disobedience as did His crucifiers. Let us observe how He speaks to us as if He is in need of us, our faith and our virtue, to relieve His agony. He loves faith for without it we cannot be saved, and He loves virtue for it is proof of our faith.

Listen and understand. Now He appears as One who needs us, but the hour is coming in which He will cease to stretch out His hand in need and we will stretch out ours instead to beg of Him. Does he who has withheld his hand from Him here, expect mercy from Him there? Listen as He says, "I have stretched out my hand and no one regarded, because you disdained all my counsel, and would have none of my rebuke, I also will laugh at your calamity; I will mock when your terror comes," (Prov 1:24,26). does he, who did not offer Him even a drop of water with which to quench His transitory thirst, expect from Him relief from eternal thirst? The rich man had asked of Abraham saying, "Have mercy on me, and send Lazarus that he may dip the tip of his finger in water and cool my tongue; for I am tormented in this flame," (Lk 16:24), but Abraham answered immediately, "between us and you there is a great gulf."

Do not harden your heart then but soften it toward Him whose heart melted as wax upon the cross for you and then you will hear Him say, "I will give of the fountain of the water of life freely to him who thirsts," (Rev 21:6).

Let your ears be attentive to this invitation, "The Spirit and the bride say, "Come!" And let him who hears say, "Come!" And let him who thirsts come. Whoever desires, let him take the water of life freely," (Rev 22:17).

THE SIXTH WORD

Amazing Victory

"It is finished" (Jn 19:30)

Our Lord Jesus Christ came to carry out two missions: spreading the Gospel and the work of redemption. When He had finished the first, He said to His Father, "I have finished the work which you have given me to do," (Jn 17:4), and when He had completed the second He said, "It is finished," (Jn 19:30).

St Augustine said that this word came as confirmation to the sayings of the prophets and as a fulfilment of all their symbols. It was as if Christ was saying, "All that has been written concerning Me by the prophets has been fulfilled," St John Chrysostom also says that these words show that the authority which had been given to devils and men over the person of Christ had ended by the death of Christ. Another contemplated that, at that time also Christ's mission in this world ended, which had caused Him hunger, thirst, fatigue, weariness, scourging and contempt. He had declared this by His saying, "I came forth from the Father and have come into the world. Again, I leave the world and go to the Father," (Jn 16:28). It was as if He was saying, "My wearisome journey is at an end and My struggle is ended. I have limited the authority of all My enemies. The great sacrifice alluded to by all other sacrifices has been accomplished, for this sacrifice is the Lamb of God, its Priest is the incarnate God, its altar the cross, its fire ardent love and its fruit the salvation of the world."

Shortly before His death, the Saviour had said, "Now is the judgment of this world; now the ruler of this world will be cast out. And I, if I am lifted up from the earth, will draw all peoples to Myself," (Jn 12:31, 32). The spiritual battle between the Saviour and Satan was carried out upon the cross. The goal of it was to restore to man the bliss of which Satan had robbed him. When the Son of God had paid the debt to His Father we were transferred from the hand of Satan to His.

In the book of Leviticus the process of the cleansing of a leper is as follows, "This shall be the law of the leper for the day of his cleansing: He shall be brought to the priest. And the priest shall go out of the camp, and the priest shall examine him; and indeed, if the leprosy is healed in the leper, then the priest shall command to take for him who is to be cleansed two living and clean birds, cedar wood, scarlet, and hyssop. And the priest shall command that one of the birds be killed in an earthen vessel over running water. As for the living bird, he shall take it, the cedar wood and the scarlet and the hyssop, and dip them and the living bird in the blood of the bird that was killed over the running water. And he shall sprinkle it seven times on him who is to be cleansed from the leprosy, and shall pronounce him clean, and shall let the living bird loose in the open field," (Lev 14:2-7). The leper, then, is man who has been expelled from Paradise, the Priest is the Lord Jesus Christ and the two birds symbolise atonement by the blood and deliverance.

In the book of Numbers, it is commanded that the manslayer who fled to the cities of refuge to be safe could not return to dwell in the land before the death of the priest (Num 35). This signifies that the sinful man has had joy restored to him after the death of Jesus Christ the High Priest. In His saying, "it is finished," we hear the tune of victory, and this tune must always be in our thoughts for then we can see that the accomplishment of His work has made our salvation possible.

Indeed our salvation would not have been possible without the work of Christ and if we wish to understand well, we must think upon the degeneration caused by our sins. It has enslaved our race, deprived us all of the freedom of a spiritual life and drawn us into the void of a dark prison with the devil its severe and eternal jailer. Every person born since the fall of Adam has become the devil's captive because he was born in sin. There was no gleam of hope nor could any tears bring about mercy and transform the devil's oppression to love. We had no power by which we could humble this tyrannical enemy and angels could not relieve us. Let us now look to Jesus for in Him alone is all hope and salvation.

His merciful eyes looked at the world and He saw between the walls of sin and His beloved and His eternal portion that the heavenly Father had given Him. He found them marred by the filth of sin and flung onto the brink of eternal doom. How could He love them and yet leave them to perish? Could He be content with entreaties for their release when divine justice calls out, "without shedding of blood there is no remission," (Heb 9:22)? He came, flying on the wings of redemptive grace, hurrying with the strength of effective might, bearing the weapons of redemptive courage, wearing upon His head the helmet of deliverance and in His hands was the price of salvation. He soared to the throne of the cross and endured the punishment of divine justice until He had "finished," all that was required.

Then the power of the devil was weakened, for the blood of Christ had paid all that was demanded and His death obliterated the enemy. The cross had smothered every doubting voice. The gates would never again be shut, the fetters were loosened, the prisoners were liberated and the tortured were redeemed, "Not with the blood of goats and calves, but with His own blood He entered the Most Holy Place once for all, having obtained eternal redemption," (Heb 9:21).

As a believer once contemplated, "Sin had prevailed upon the earth and the water had flooded it but could not wash away the sickness of sin. The fire fell from heaven upon it but could not burn away transgression. The earth opened up but could not swallow the wickedness. The Law came with all its thunderous threats from the midst of the darkness on Mount Sinai but could not terrify the sons of transgression. Sin continued to thrive till it dared to spread its tents on Golgotha and nailed the Lawgiver to the wood, but it left Him battle wounded and dying. So the beaten and overpowered Sacrifice became the Victorious."

"It is finished," is a comprehensive and comforting word. This cry is one of victory and it means that the will of God was fulfilled, the salvation of mankind guaranteed and eternal victory won. Heaven has opened to man and the darkness of the grave has been transformed to the glory of resurrection and ascension with Christ. The invitation has been sent and the guest has won the privilege. Though we were unable to pay the price for this invitation ourselves we passed it on to a Person who was united with us, and we became as Levi was in the loins of Abraham (Heb 7:10).

Indeed, Christ fell but in so doing He has crushed His enemies, "Whoever falls on that stone will be broken; but on whomever it falls, it will grind him to powder," (Lk 20:18). He died for sin but He has crucified sin and death to His cross. He was inundated by suffering but He left wickedness in its depth and came out unscathed. He was surrounded by the fire of pain but He left transgression behind in it to be devoured by it and it was unable to singe Him. Fear not, my brethren, no matter the fears from within and the wars from without for you have been reconciled through the blood of Jesus, "For if when we were enemies we were reconciled to God through the death of His Son, much more, having been reconciled, we shall be saved by His life," (Rom 5:10).

As someone once said, "Through His death we have crossed the Red Sea by night. Through His life we have crossed the Jordan River by day. Through His death we have been saved from the iron forge in Egypt. Through His life we have been saved from all the perils of the wilderness. Through His death He was victorious over Pharaoh the chief enemy. Through His life He will triumph over Sihon, king of the Amorites and Og, king of Bashan. We will be saved through His life. As He lives, we will also live. Have confidence that the work has been accomplished and redemption perfected. The kingdom of heaven has been opened to all believers and He has taken those who have slept to Paradise. So lift up your heads you prisoners of hope, for there is no debt that has not been paid, no devil not defeated and no enemy within your hearts not wounded with a deadly wound, "But thanks be to God, who gives us the victory through our Lord Jesus Christ," (I Cor 15:57)."

From this day your situation is in the hand of your Saviour Christ and the authority of Satan and the slavery of sin have ended. The compensation has been offered and the justification accomplished. Salvation and eternal life have been acquired and the agreement for freedom has been stamped. So spread the news, you prisoners and be delighted you captives.

How exhilarating was the sound of the shouting on the day of the Jubilee for the weary of Israel and beautiful was its ring in their ears. How strong was their yearning to hear the sounding of the trumpets of the priests as they waited to be liberated. But here there is a voice that can be heard from on the cross from the great Chief Priest, "It is finished," What could be more beautiful than that voice - a voice of joy for sinners, "The voice of rejoicing and salvation," (Ps 118:15).

Christ has atoned for sin, but if you see someone enslaved to sin, then this is his choice. This situation will be as if a rich man had gone to buy captives with a generous amount and then proceeded to provide them with ships, horses and provisions to liberate them from their captivity. Some, however, refused to leave after he had paid for their freedom. So it is with Christ Who has prepared for sinners ships of deliverance and mounts of salvation but they refused to be rescued and rejected salvation, "To whom He said, "This is the rest with which you may cause the weary to rest," and, "This is the refreshing"; Yet they would not hear," (Is 28:12).

With his own free will, man had thrown the reins of his soul between the hands of Satan and so Satan had lawfully received it. It was then necessary that it be retrieved from him in a just way and so God would atone for the disobedient through His Son. He was able to return to the soul of man its lost freedom. Why then do we see many who are still captive to sin, yielding to Satan. This freewill that God created man with and with which he surrendered himself to Satan, is left to him and God will not oppose him surrendering himself to Satan once more. Those who returned with Ezra the priest from the Babylonian captivity were few compared to those remained behind. Those who refused to return represent those who persist in their sins and are attached to this futile world without faith in their beloved Redeemer. To those St Paul says, "Stand fast therefore in the liberty by which Christ has made us free, and do not be entangled again with a yoke of bondage," (Gal 5:1).

Gaze, O my soul, at that cross, and while you look, listen to the great cry, "It is finished". The great work is ended. Jesus has completed all things. From now on all He asks of the sinner is to believe in the Achiever of this great redemption. Christ has completed all that is required and he who knows this truth has attained peace with God. If then you do not have this peace, it is because you have not believed in His saying, "It is finished."

Trust that He has paid all your debts and then you will not be able to hold back the outburst of peace within yourself. The blood is the means of reconciliation and your peace is the certain outcome of the effectiveness of this blood. If you ponder, my beloved, this unlimited reconciliation guaranteed by this blood, you will then be entitled to say, "Peace is mine!"

THE SEVENTH WORD

Amazing Death

"Father, 'into Your hands I commit My spirit" (Lk 23:46)

These were the last word spoken by Jesus before He died. Many of the dying words spoken by famous people are remembered but none of these words convey the same trust and tranquillity as these words do.

He began and ended His words on the cross with the word "Father". He calls God Father and yet has obeyed Him even unto the death of the cross. In Christ's death His full obedience to His Father was manifested, for there is nothing dearer to a person than his soul, and the Son of God offered Himself willingly submitting to the will of His Father. He offered it not only for His friends and loved ones but also for His enemies, for sinners and for those who have denied His kindness. This He did so that He may save them from hell and render them His brothers and members in the heavenly kingdom. The joy of the Son was great for He had entrusted what was dearest to Him into the hands of His Father and would reclaim them shortly. About this St Paul says, "Who, in the days of His flesh, when He had offered up prayers and supplications, with vehement cries and tears to Him who was able to save Him from death, and was heard because of His godly fear," (Heb 5:7).

What spirit left its body so victorious as this spirit did? There has never been a last breath, to be emitted in such a majestic and impressive manner as that of the Saviour. His spirit had left His body without fear but rather it left triumphantly and so terrified the powers of darkness. People's determination generally wanes and weakens as they enter the door of death no matter their might but Christ had His life as in the prophecy, "He will not quarrel nor cry out, Nor will anyone hear His voice in the streets," (Matt 21:19). He was neither mighty nor powerful until He wished to expend His last breath.

Now the mysterious darkness that had hidden the face of the Father from Him earlier dissipated. Now the painful feeling that He had been left alone vanished. Now He had come to the end and cried out with all certainty that the Father had not left Him.

No human has the strength to raise his voice at the time of his death but the Saviour had cried out, "with a loud voice," (Matt 27:50), indicating that He is the Lord and Prince of life (Act 3:15).

What do we learn then from these words, "Father, 'into Your hands I commit My spirit," (Lk 23:46)? That the obedience of Christ, to His Father, His entire life is what gave Him confidence at His death. If we walk in His way, then, we will rise to heaven in peace and enjoy His glory. If we follow in the footsteps of our divine Teacher, by obeying the will of our heavenly Father, we will attain true glory. We should understand that the obedience of Christ was a practical obedience. If we want to obey the Lord, then we should obey Him in deeds, thoughts and words.

At the time of its departure from the body, the spirit of Christ was:

I. Powerful

Many times the power of the spirit overcomes the weakness of the body. Whoever departs this life, after virtuous living will have this experience. They will have strength to overcome death. The sensitivity of spirit will be proportional to the weakness of the body to feel at the time of death either the sweetness of goodness or the bitterness of wickedness, as the case may be.

Let us then avoid wickedness lest our spirits taste its bitterness at the time of our departure. Which do you plant then, a tree of righteousness or a tree of iniquity? "For whatever a man sows, that he will also reap. For he who sows to his flesh will of the flesh reap corruption, but he who sows to the Spirit will of the Spirit reap everlasting life," (Gal 6:7,8).

2. Victorious Over its Enemies

The believer will sense the pleasure of victory over his spiritual enemies upon his death. He will know the extent of the peril he was exposed to and the strength of his enemies that did battle with him, and he will rejoice and be astounded. He will rejoice at the victory and be amazed at how he had escaped considering his weakness and the enormity of the dangers. He will sing, as the Israelites did on the seashore, and say, "I will sing to the LORD, For He has triumphed gloriously! The horse and its rider He has thrown into the sea! The LORD is my strength and song, And He has become my salvation; He is my God, and I will praise Him; My father's God, and I will exalt Him," (Ex 15:1-2). Indeed, Lord, You are the One who has endowed me with victory, so let me rely on You and on no one else.

Defeat is not that of forces in battle and combat, but that of the defeat of the evil spirit at death. As much as the believer rejoices at his victory, the wicked will burn with grief at his defeat.

3. Happy

Happy that it has completed its work and has not spent even

one minute other than in doing good. He who spends his life in dutiful work does not appreciate his worth or rejoice in it, as he should, until the time of his death. How many, as their death approaches, become disturbed and anxious at the knowledge that they have lived a life disobeying the will of their God? Nothing overcomes the fear at the time of death except true faith that has remained with a person because of his obedience to his heavenly Father.

What reassured Christ at the time of His death was His knowledge that He had not spent His life wastefully. To each person is one life - if he employs it in attachment to the world, he will feel that he has lost it forever. This is the cause of the fear of death. However, he who spends his life in the fear of God has "a refuge in his death," (Prov 14:32). St Paul cries out victoriously before his death saying, "I have fought the good fight, I have finished the race, I have kept the faith. Finally, there is laid up for me the crown of righteousness," (2 Tim 4:7-8).

The wicked tremble when death comes at the knowledge that it will severe the thread of their earthly existence and throw them in the depths of pain. This manner of death, however, does not assault the believer, but it approaches him as a cheerful friend and it opens the cage of the body that his joyful spirit may fly out quickly to the embrace of the Redeemer.

The slaves of Satan fear the grave for they are sure that in it they will receive the wages of sin. The faithful, however hear the exultant voice saying, "I will ransom them from the power of the grave," (Hos 13:14).

Let all the faithful remember this and let them prepare to surrender their spirits into the hands of their heavenly Father, knowing that no enemy can snatch it from there. It cannot be concealed that the situation between death and eternity is very critical, so we must muster all our senses and all our faith and trust in God and offer it to Him along with our souls. We must not be anxious then but we must repeat Christ's blessed words, "Father, 'into Your hands I commit My spirit,'" then accept death and our judgment willingly.

The surrender of all that we have at the time of departure is the best preparation for death. Do not fear the raising of this barrier from between - that is the barrier of the body that veils the face of God as it is. Do not worry about surrendering it to worms and corruption, submitting it rather to divine will. Whenever we submit in this respect, we throw ourselves upon the endless sea of divine mercy so that even sins, of all kind, that the devil will try to recall at the hour of death will seem as a tiny spot that does not cause the least disturbance.

At that time, do not look except to the cross of Christ and the worthiness of the Son of God the Redeemer. The drops of His blood will wash away your transgression and His cross will become for you a ladder on which your spirit will ascend to eternal repose. Do not rely on your works or look to it as if it qualifies you for the heavenly kingdom, for your works without the blood of Christ are like a tattered rag. Lean with all your strength upon the cross in doing the pleasure of your Redeemer and the fulfilment of His law. If you reach the gate to heaven then only enter it through the name of Jesus where you will be completely welcomed in the eternal abode.

Ponder well the word of Christ, for the expression, "Father," indicates absolute love and the expression, "I commit", proves the fullness of hope, reliance and acceptance of what God plans.

The expression, "My spirit," points to all that is dear, beloved and precious. If you look at the abundance of your sins at the time of your passing, raise your head above and contemplate the worthiness of Christ and you will find a cure for your fears.

Everything, no matter how great, is worthless compared to Christ and if God has sacrificed His Only-Begotten Son, will He then withhold from us the forgiveness of our offences? Strengthen your faith then and trust that God will forgive all your lapses. If He has commanded us to forgive our trespassers seventy times seven times, is He then less merciful than us? Do not despair or lose hope but depend on the mercy and compassion of God.

How much thanks is due to the Lord Jesus for He has opened wide before us the door of mercy. Hades can only show you the dark prison and to reveal to you the suffering and hardship that Christ has saved you from. He will reveal to you on the morning of the day of the resurrection, which has no night, the exultation of your happiness that was bought for you by the blood of Christ the Redeemer.

CHAPTER 11

Jesus Gives up His Spirit

"And bowing His head, He gave up His spirit" (Jn 19:30)

Jesus gave up His spirit into the hands of His father and died. Behold the Son dies. The Living loses His life. He who has raised the dead surrenders His spirit into the hand of the Father. The beloved Son dies. Behold the Sun of righteousness sets atop Golgotha. The Tree of Life bows His head and takes the pose of death and dies.

O you sinners, your Saviour has died. You righteous your Justifier has died. O you poor He, who satisfies you, is dead. Your protector, O children, is dead. You wretched He, who had compassion on you, is dead. Your comforter is dead, O you who mourn. Grieve for Him all of you and ask Him not to prolong the time of His absence from you, and say with Him, "For You will not leave my soul in Sheol, Nor will You allow Your Holy One to see corruption," (Ps 16:10).

Look, O believer, to your Lord as He surrenders His spirit into the hands of His Father and if you see Him bowing His head, do not be like the Jews who imagined that they had destroyed His kingdom by crucifying Him. He whom you see before you now bowing the head will be seen by the multitude of believers who have faith in Him as King. Those martyrs, whose blood was shed for His glory, will also be seen weaving for Him His eternal purple royal robe. His golden sceptre will be seen to crush all the earthly kings.

His enemies thought that He was alone, though in the world He has a flock that loves Him as a Father and serves Him as a King and worships Him as a God. No one could be capable of changing or diminishing the greatness of His honour in generations to come.

If you see your Saviour cry out with a loud voice and give up

His spirit, know that He turns heavenward and offers Himself to the Father as the Lamb caught in the thicket, prepared to be in Isaac's place as an offering and as the new Adam harvesting the thorns and thistles from the cursed ground and finally as Christ to whom Israel (the unfruitful vineyard) offered a bramble though He is the Master who comes to harvest the fruit. Since He is the atoning Sacrifice and the King of the future, He offered His glorious head, adorned with a bloodied crown as a sun with its rays. Beneath this radiant crown, the darkness could not stop the gaze of the righteous or the love of God or His greatness from enlivening their hearts.

Indeed grace has established its throne upon the virtue of the suffering of the Redeemer. He seized His golden sceptre and uncovered the realm of the ruler of darkness and so the doors of that formidable grave were opened and new life stirred in the midst of its weary inhabitants as eternity began to wander in the midst of the graves.

He raised His voice while He was dying, "and the graves were opened; and many bodies of the saints who had fallen asleep were raised," (Matt 27:52). His death was accompanied by the resurrection of the dead. Has there ever been another whose death enables the dead to live? As long as the grave was open it received its victims, who had no refuge and when it seized them it did not return them. "There are three things that are never satisfied, Four never say, "Enough!": The grave,

The barren womb, The earth that is not satisfied with water—And the fire never says, "Enough!" (Prov 30:15-16). The grave was never satiated but at the death of Christ, it opened up and restored its victims in obedience to Him, for by death He conquered death.

St Jacob of Serug said, "By what death were the dead made to move and rise up from their graves? Before whom of the dead did the walls of Hades fall? Who is He that kicked the graves so that they threw up their dead? Who is this who flung destruction upon the fertile land of death? Who is this dead One who was tied and crucified between thieves and then released those who are bound in darkness? Who of the dead is this One who gave the new life and at whose entrance the valley of the dead trembled? Who is this who accepted the crown of thorns and was crucified and bore the crown of death that it may not reign?"

The Saviour said, "Most assuredly, I say to you, unless a grain of wheat falls into the ground and dies, it remains alone; but if it dies, it produces much grain," (Jn 12:24). The death of the Son of God bore the fruit of eternal life, "that He might bring us to God, being put to death in the flesh but made alive by the Spirit," (I Pet 3:18). He tasted death that He may bequeath eternal life to us. As when the first Adam ate from the first forbidden fruit and brought death upon all his offspring, so the Second Adam, that is Christ, came and tasted the bitter fruit, the fruit of death, that He may endow the whole of humanity with life eternal.

The Master continued to swallow the bitterness of divine and human suffering until He finished and surrendered His spirit and thus sealed this critical event. Hear O sinners news that will strengthen your flight - He bowed His head. Witness the King of the heavens dying. He who created the universe was incarnate and this incarnate God surrenders His spirit. Meditate upon Him and hope for a certain salvation. Have faith in Christ. Throw yourselves between His hands. Take Him and believe that He is all in all and throw your trembling hands around that bloodied body. Sit beneath that cross. Touch that precious blood and kiss

His holy wounds, for from them flowed the springs of grace and by them the smears of transgression and sin were washed and the cursed Earth was purified.

Where sin abounded for judgement, grace abounded for justification. Where sin flourished for filthiness, grace flourished for cleansing. Where sin thrived for ruthlessness, grace thrived for submission and temperance. Where sin increased for the captivity of mankind, grace increased for the liberation of the captives. Where sin, that violates the law and offends its Giver, multiplied, so much more grace came to repair the breach and erase the stain. Where sin grew for the annihilation of the soul by an unquenchable fire and with worms that do not die, grace grew further for the quenching of the fire and the healing of the wounds.

God has enabled many to know this glorious revelation of the Redeemer in the time and gravity of death. Isaiah was able to discern through that very body, lacerated with torture, the Man of suffering and to value the blood that had covered it as undeniable proof that He had gone through the anguish of divine displeasure to alone achieve salvation. David seeing the wounds of His hands and feet, counting His bare bones and perceiving the traces of vinegar and gall on His lips, was able to know that He was his descendant and Christ. During the general unrest of elements and souls, Daniel was able to know the abomination of desolation. Ezekiel, Joel, Malachi and Moses all were enabled to see and honour the voluntary sacrifice of the Lord.

Considering His ancestry Jesus was a King and the epitaph placed above His head cried out saying that though the royal sceptre had come to an end in Judah, it has been picked up again by Christ, the awaited by all nations and the One who has opened up His kingdom to all from that moment on. Abraham, Isaac, Noah and Shem could not deny their seed and the subject of their faith. It was not left to Adam but to shelter behind the Seed of the woman who had bruised the head of the serpent. They all came out of their graves and passed before the wood of shame immersed with blood, for they needed to confirm that the mystery of redemption had been accomplished by reaching their hands out to the Sacrifice.

Furthermore, some of those living saw the finger of God in this moving scene free from the troubled nature. The Centurion who was in charge of the Roman soldiers was moved before all the rest and said, "Certainly this was a righteous Man!" (Lk 23:47) and along with the others he uttered, "Truly this was the Son of God!" (Matt 27:45). So Jesus had barely been lifted off the earth and yet had drawn to Himself the first fruits of the nations.

But come and be amazed! Did His death affect His crucifiers? The rocks were moved for Him but the hearts of sinners did not soften. He had died but they not only still hated Him but also assaulted His pure body. When Alexander the Great, who had struggled long to defeat Darius of Persia, saw his dead body after he had been killed, he was shocked at the spectacle before him and then he was overwhelmed with grief. He wept bitterly. He then spread his own military cloak over the dead body and arranged for it to be laid in a very costly coffin. In contrast, the body of the Lord Jesus Christ, though dead, nailed and wounded was attacked by one of soldiers with a spear, so that the side was opened and the heart pierced.

But He who had defeated His slaughterers with His patience, triumphed over him who had pierced Him by His death. Has it been heard of that the dead can defeat the living? "Immediately blood and water came out," (Jn 19:34). Examine that spear and you will find it covered in blood. Thanks to God that the blood had covered up the offence. As was foretold by the prophet, "In that day a fountain shall be opened for the house of David and for the inhabitants of Jerusalem, for sin and for uncleanness," (Zech 13:1). So now the fountain that purifies sin and uncleanness has been opened. Come all you who thirst and draw water and drink freely. The waters have erupted from the Rock, let the people drink and be quenched forever.

"He placed cherubim at the east of the garden of Eden, and a flaming sword which turned every way, to guard the way to the tree of life," (Gen.3:24). St Jacob of Serug noted, "Jesus came to enter Paradise with His cross but the guard heard it and pierced Him with his spear. He received the spear in His side and opened for all to enter. They opened His side that all sinners may enter heaven. Blood and water came out of it. A new well has sprung on Golgotha. Blood flood out to show that He is alive and water to show that He is dead. Who but the Lord can be both alive and dead! Our Redeemer has shed blood from His heart also that the world may see the greatness of His love, as His pure blood was shed to the last drop."

Rise, then, from your slumber O my soul, and witness the blood and the water flowing out of the side of the beloved Saviour onto the ground. Kiss them with your lips that they may be purified and address Him with those lips that have been purified with the blood and water flowing from Him saying, "Make me worthy, my Saviour, to enter to You from this open side that it may surround me, possess me and veil me from all that is in the world of vainglory and fleeting comfort. Do not allow me to turn another but You and let my only song, all the days of my life here on earth be, "My eyes are upon You, O GOD the Lord," (Ps 141:8).

Gaze at the cross - what do you see? You will see the Lord dead but this dead Lord is the Ruler of life. Life exists with Him. He died but it was you who should have died. He died that He may lift death from you and may give you eternal life. His death is life to sinners and without this death there is no life for the dead but sin.

Let us all then address our Saviour saying," Our beloved Saviour, every time we see You bowing Your head and yielding Your spirit, we are comforted and encouraged confident in our salvation. We entrust ourselves to You, not only at the hour of death, but from now on do not allow us to be separated from You for one moment. If we look at Your body covered in wounds, let us be filled with the knowledge of the greatness of Your love and the enormity of our betrayal. You have loved us but how often do we treat You callously with our sins? How many times does Your pure blood call out to us to rise from our sins but we remain in them? Woe to you sinner who scorns this God you see hanging on the cross for your sake.

CHAPTER 12

Jesus is Buried

"Now behold, there was a man named Joseph, a council member, a good and just man. He had not consented to their decision and deed. He was from Arimathea, a city of the Jews, who himself was also waiting for the kingdom of God. This man went to Pilate and asked for the body of Jesus. Then he took it down, wrapped it in linen, and laid it in a tomb that was hewn out of the rock, where no one had ever lain before"

(Lk 23 50-53)

Let us meditate now on how the Lord was taken down from the cross. The importance of friends and loved ones is revealed in times of adversity and there is no adversity for man like death. True friendship appears after death. So who cared for our Saviour upon His death and who remained by the cross until His burial? St Matthew the evangelist informs us that Mary Magdalene, Mary the mother of James and Josses and the mother of Zebedee's sons, along with many other women were at the cross after His death (Matt 27:55-56). St John also mentions that he himself had witnessed the piercing of Jesus with the spear after His death and the mother of the Saviour was with Him (Jn 19: 35). But how can these frail people manage to take the body of Jesus down from the cross to bury Him? A rich man from Arimathea called Joseph, who himself also was a disciple of Jesus, went to Pilate and asked for the body of Jesus.

In Pilate's famous Report to Tiberius Caesar, he describes his state after the crucifixion of Christ, "I returned to the Praetorium, sad and pensive. On ascending the stairs, the steps of which were still stained with the blood of the Nazarene, I perceived an old man in a suppliant posture, and behind him several Romans in tears. He threw himself at my feet and wept most bitterly. It is painful to see an old man weep, and my heart being already overcharged with grief, we though strangers wept together. And in truth it seemed that the tears lay very shallow that day with many whom I perceived, in the vast concourse of people. I never witnessed such an extreme revulsion of feeling. Those who betrayed and sold him, those who testified against him, those who cried, "Crucify him, we want his blood," all slunk off like cowardly curs and washed their teeth with vinegar. As I am told that Jesus taught a resurrection after death, if such be the fact, also a separation, I am sure it commenced in the vast crowd. "Father," said I to him, after gaining control of my feelings, "who are you, and what is your request," "I am Joseph of Arimathea," replied he, "and am come to beg of you upon my knees the permission to bury Jesus of Nazareth," "Your prayer is granted," said I to him, and at the same time I ordered Manlius to take some soldiers with him to superintend the entombment, lest it should be profaned."

Yes, this is how the Saviour was brought down from the cross into the hands of a few friends. Chivalry did not move any of those who were expected at that time. Yes, none of His disciples, or His loved ones who had gathered together after his resurrection to await the Holy Spirit, or the over five hundred brethren to whom He appeared could be found to care for Him. No one witnessed the burial of the Saviour except for a very small number of His disciples and the faithful. Thomas who had said, "Let us also go, that we may die with Him", was not in their midst, nor was Peter who had said, "Even if I have to die with You, I will not deny You", nor the scribe who had said, "Teacher, I will follow You wherever You go," (Matt 8:19).

How many thousands did He bless and show kindness to, and yet not one of them came at the time of His shrouding? How quickly does a person extend their hands to receive goodness from God and then how quickly does he close them again when goodness is asked of him. Yes, none of the sick who had been healed were there at His burial. It was right for the withered hand that had been restored to be extended before any other to remove the nails from His hands and feet. Yet this person and many others like him, were absent at that hour, to teach us that those who feel the grace of the Lord are those who have a genuine appreciation of His blessings. For He shines His sun upon the righteous and the wicked but amongst those on whom He bestows blessings, are many who blaspheme Him, neglect Him and despise His worship.

The Saviour had once cured ten lepers but only one returned to thank Him, so that He said, "Were there not ten cleansed? But where are the nine?" (Lk 17:17). When John, Joseph, Nicodemus and some of the women were taking down the body of Christ from the cross, His state seemed to cry out, "Are these all that have come to declare their gratitude for My goodness toward them? I have healed many, so where are they? I have fed thousands, so why are they absent? I have relieved the agony of a great number of the suffering, so why are they late? Where are My disciples? Where are all those I have shown goodness? In every generation, I have not withheld My grace from anyone, but the grateful are few."

It is for us now to contemplate the condition of His mother at His burial. Someone once imagined that once they had taken the body of Jesus down off the cross, His affectionate mother took Him and hugged Him and kissed Him with great reverence and washed Him with her tears and took the crown of thorns of His head, and with great caution removed the nails from his hands and feet. Then she pondered His wounds and said, "O holy wounds! You are still open for all who desire to take refuge in You."

From there they carried Christ to be buried. Let us follow St Mary as she witnesses her Son being placed in the tomb. It is hard for a mother to stand by the bed of her ailing son and not suffer along with Him. How much more was the suffering of the mother of Jesus as she observed them placing Him in the tomb? No doubt she was remembering happier times and spoke to herself saying, "Where have those days of Bethlehem gone, when the heavens rejoiced at the birth of the Son of God and the shepherds and the Magi came to praise and worship Him?"

Another contemplated; "Jesus wrote His will while on the cross: He gave his garment to the soldier, His mother to John, His spirit to His Father and His body to the grave."

While the rays of the sun were setting and hiding behind the mountains, the Lord of life was lying in the tomb between the folds of the shroud. While all this was happening, every family had slaughtered the Passover lamb and was preparing to eat it without realising that the Sacrifice of Golgotha had abolished the need for all these offerings and that from that moment on salvation was in Jesus alone, for He alone was the Prince of life. So you, beloved of Christ, do not fear, for He whom you now see entering Hades must do battle with His enemies there, prevail and rise triumphant and victorious.

St Jacob of Serug said, "Adam went down to the grave, so the Son of God went down after him. He turned the dust of the dead and sought him in the midst of the ruin. Death had reigned and bound the tribes of the earth with a crown and no one was able to loosen this crown of death. For this reason the Lord entered the place of death to destroy death and to release Adam from its power. When He entered, He took on the garment of the dead and their colour in order to call upon them. The Light shone upon the sorrowing and gladdened them and the silenced mouths began to shout in glory. The Lion roared in Hades, death heard Him and the miserable one trembled and his crown fell in the darkness."

If Christ had not suffered, died and been buried for our sakes, we would not have had comfort at death. The thought of being placed in the grave is very terrible indeed but Jesus died and was buried for our sakes so that we may not fear death.

Then, let every believer say, "Welcome to the grave, I will not live there forever. Jesus was there before me, so I will not fear darkness. There I will rest till He raises me. I will welcome Him for He will come with a brilliant victory."

Let us meditate upon the death and burial of our Saviour, for the angels desire to look into it (1 Pet 1:12) and if our eyes are opened then as the eyes of Elisha's servant were, (2 Kings 6:17), we will see multitudes of angels amongst those standing before the cross, gazing astounded at the scene before them. The Son of God hangs on the cross! They are amazed that He whom "the heaven of heavens cannot contain," (1 King 8:27) is now being placed in a small tomb. Are we able to grasp this strange scene? If the door of heaven is opened, will people not yearn greatly to gaze at it and to see the wonders of Paradise? Only, the matter is the reverse of what was related for we would see a small window in heaven open to this fallen world and the angels above looking toward earth, as if there was no subject in heaven to attract their attention as that of Christ and His salvation.

So contemplate, my soul, that which the angels contemplated. Contemplate the precious hands that had fed the thousands in the wilderness and that had held the sick and raised them whole. Behold His feet that had walked on water. His feet that Mary had anointed with the fragrant oil and wiped with her hair and now are still. Now the hands and the feet are wrapped in the shroud. Look at Him as He is placed in the tomb and left there to sleep. It is a hard thing for the mind to comprehend.

Who am I, my God, that You should surrender Your Son to death for my sake? Am I not a contemptible worm who has offended You with my wicked deeds and has deserved Your anger and displeasure?

You, my good Saviour, Who died to give me life and Who shed Your blood to wash away with it my sins, give me to look to You on the cross dying out of love for us. Give me to see Your cross as the throne of Your glory and death as the voice of your love. Love then is upon His throne. Let us remain, then, upon that cross and die with our good Saviour, to be satisfied with His love and to be worthy to sit with Him upon His throne.

The beloved said in Songs, "When I found the one I love. I held him and would not let him go," (Song 3:4). The women had clung to Him strongly when they had met Him after the resurrection (Matt 28:9). Cling to Him then, O my soul and let my hands hold Him firmly. Let not my eyes turn from seeing Him or my ears from hearing Him. Forget, my heart, all but Jesus. Ignite within me, my Saviour, Your love that I may live and die in Your embrace and that I may commend my spirit to Your pure hands.

Let us kiss the pierced feet of our Saviour and His holy wounds. Why do we not regret our sins when we see Him suffering for our sakes? Do we despise His love? Do we disdain His blood? Let us crucify our wills with Him on the cross so that we may not abandon the place of our peace or the spring of our joy.

CHAPTER 13

On the Necessity of the Efficacy of Christ's Death for Salvation

"For if by the one man's offense many died, much more the grace of God and the gift by the grace of the one Man, Jesus Christ, abounded to many"

(Rom 5:15)

Consider, O man, that our salvation would not have been possible except through the death of Christ. The Son of God was incarnate to bring about our redemption and we could not be justly redeemed in any other way, for sin is infinite when committed against an infinite God. It was not in the capacity of man to pay the debt due to the boundless gulf between God and man. So it became necessary that He who would pay the debt would be of limitless honour, esteem and equal in every respect to Him toward whom the offence was committed.

A theologian once put it this way, "Let us suppose that a servant had slapped a king or had struck with a rod. It is certain then, that no matter what punishment is imposed by the king, it will never suffice to wipe out the guilt for the existence of the great gulf between the worth of the honourable king and the lowly servant. What parity could exist between the king's offence and the servant's suffering or death and how can the payment be sufficient unless the offender is equal rank and importance to the offended and is willing to offer in compensation all that is imposed upon him as restoration for his insult and atonement for his offence?

So we find that wretched man, who is of no more value than dust or a worm, has offended the King of glory through his sins. Had God killed him the offence would not have been eliminated. It was imperative that the Man be equal to God and to accept for Himself the punishment and the atonement for the guilt.

But God has shown His abundant mercy and arranged a marvellous plan by which to forgive man and to pay what was owed His divine justice. When God saw that man could not pay the debt, He incarnated and placed Himself under the sentence necessitated by man's sin.

If someone should ask saying that we deserved to suffer forever but Christ suffered for a short while, how then can His brief suffering correspond to what we deserve to suffer eternally? We answer saying firstly, that we should remember Who it is that suffers in our stead and look to the majesty of His person and secondly that the sinner deserves unlimited punishment because the extent of the sin is immeasurable but human capacity for suffering is limited and no matter how much the suffering he would still be unable to atone for himself or for another.

But our dear Redeemer is the vessel of the immeasurable divine love. He was able to truly feel the weight of sin before God and to suffer the consequences to an immeasurable extent and an imaginable depth. On the one hand He knew God fully and all that divine glory required. On the other hand, He knew sin was exorbitant and offensive to God and since He was without sin, He was able to take it upon Himself and to endure it until justice was accomplished. God could not accept mankind without atonement. If He had pardoned them, where would have been holiness and truth for He had declared that sin was deplorable to Him and that He would not acquit the guilty yet, if He had truly destroyed them where would have been love? Thanks to God forever for He found a way to exonerate the wanton and remain righteous. As St Paul said, "whom God set forth as a propitiation by His blood, through faith, to demonstrate His righteousness, because in His forbearance God had passed over the sins that were previously committed, to demonstrate at the present time His righteousness, that He might be just and the justifier of the one who has faith in Jesus," (Rom 3:25-26).

The objective behind the death of Christ is to find unity

between hatred of sin and the compassion on and affection for sinners. He showed an approach that was just to His attributes, law and guidelines and merciful to us wretched men.

You sinner seeking salvation, search for Him everywhere, you will not find Him until you come to the cross and there you will say, "We have found the Messiah," (which is translated, the Christ)," (Jn 1:41). There you will not be able to restrain yourself from crying out, "Behold! The Lamb of God who takes away the sin of the world!" (Jn 1:29), knowing your sin is in this collective sin. Approach Him without fear for He has prepared to reveal His glory just as He had prepared for salvation.

The cross of Christ is the power of God for salvation from eternal destruction. There is, however, another enemy that should be feared and that enemy is sin. If man is not saved from sin he will not find a heaven. God has placed the way of salvation from sin in His cross. The objective behind the death of Christ then is not just to rescue us from the punishment but also from sin and its consequences. St Paul says, "who gave Himself for us, that He might redeem us from every lawless deed and purify for Himself His own special people, zealous for good works," (Ti 2:14).

Christ died to change the heart of fallen and stubborn man who loves the pleasures of this evil world, to His original image and so qualify him to partake in the divine nature (2 Peter 1:4). Look, you anxious sinner, to Jesus Christ for in Him you will find all you need and He will become for you wisdom, righteousness and redemption (1 Cor 1:20).

On what foundation do you rely on deliverance from sin? Listen to what the Apostle says, "For no other foundation can anyone lay than that which is laid, which is Jesus Christ," (1Cor

3:11). Trust in Jesus alone to be delivered from your sins. If you have struggled much with your own strength to free yourself from sin and have failed, listen to these comforting words: "My grace is sufficient for you, for My strength is made perfect in weakness," (2Cor 12:9). These words are sufficient to will carry you to the arms of Christ the crucified. Realise that He is covered in blood for you and He suffered pain with no personal gain for your sake, that you may acquire life.

No doubt that when you contemplate your many sins, you feel that it is not your destiny to approach the presence of God and when you gaze into the attributes of the just God, it seems to you that your many sins are as hard thorns ready to pierce and stab your members but do not worry about this as long as you see that Jesus Christ has died in your place. Yes divine justice has acceded to a throne of fire but before that throne another has been placed for the cross of Christ that overflows with peace that it may hide in its shadow the anxious sinner.

Stand beneath the cross of Christ calling out saying, "O Lamb of God who shed His blood for my sake, Your death is a miracle of mercy that fills all of heaven with amazement. Give me to believe that You have saved me from eternal punishment and that You will save me from sin so that I may become a new creation. I desire to live for You but am not strong enough for that unless I depend on Your cross. Let me not trust in anything else but Your sacrifice. Let me sing Your words "My grace is sufficient for you," and chant saying "Let Your mercies come also to me, O LORD—Your salvation according to Your word," (Ps 119:41).

Fix your eyes upon the cross of Christ and nowhere else, as the devil expends his efforts in blinding people to the meaning of the cross, for if they paid attention to it they would find in it a trusted refuge for them. Do not place a veil of self-sufficiency upon your eyes that will hide the glory of the cross from you and delay you from coming to the Spring of Life. Remember the brass serpent that Moses raised by God's command, that all who had been bitten may look at it and live. Observe those bitten and witness how they peer at that serpent that aids in their healing. They do no turn their sights away from the brass serpent till they see a new sun in the sky. Their eyes were fixed on what they believed possessed healing. This should also be your custom, O sinner. Look to Jesus, for with Him there is healing and whenever we gaze with our eyes of faith at the cross that has been raised so that all that believe in Him should not perish but have everlasting life, our sense of healing and deliverance from sin will grow.

Sit and observe the Saviour dying that the faith may be formed in your heart willingly and obediently. There is no place equal to Golgotha in the establishment of faith in the heart. Truly, the breeze from that holy mound blows over a weak and anxious faith with the scent of strength and constancy and grants the heart of the believer the sweetness of a new life that removes for him the bitterness of death. How many of the faithful have visited this holy place and proclaimed their delight from enjoying the nectar of faith.

Truly the cross is the rod of wonders that brings forth water from the rock, so beware that you do not doubt its efficacy in your salvation from sin. Know that the suffering of Jesus is sufficient for your salvation and that of the whole world considering its immensity. Do not think of repeating this tragedy with your lack of appreciation and do not place the crown of thorns on His head with your doubts in His ability and your dependence on your own.

Ask of Him to remove from you this spirit of pride, the spirit of dependence on one's weak self, the spirit of seeking deliverance from sin through your own personal strength. Depend on the merit of Christ's death for your salvation and say, "Here I am, Lord, a tree between Your hands. Plant me in the field of grace, water me with Your pure blood and grant that I bear fruit worthy of repentance."

CHAPTER 14

The Meaning of the Cross

"But God demonstrates His own love toward us, in that while we were still sinners, Christ died for us" (Rom 5:8)

Since the beginning of time, God has declared His love for mankind in many different ways, and wants us to be sure of His love always. For this reason He continues to remind us through His acts of love. In the Old Testament, all His words were confined to the rebuke of mankind over the hardness of their hearts and the reminder of His love for them. He showed them that all His works demonstrated this love and that He did not deserve all this callousness but that they should return the love He has first shown them.

The more the Lord worked toward winning the hearts of men, the more they persisted in drawing away from Him. Finally He resolved to reveal His love in a more perfect and complete way that would enable Him to change and soften their hearts and to draw them to Himself, "In this the love of God was manifested toward us, that God has sent his only begotten Son into the world, that we might live through Him," (I Jn 4:9).

The owner of the vineyard sent the vinedressers prophets in order to declare His love for them but they did not listen to them and killed them. He then sent His beloved Son so that when they saw Him they might appreciate His compassion and say: "For God so loved the world that He gave His only begotten Son, that whoever believes in Him should not perish but have everlasting life," (Jn 3:16), and, "He loved us and sent His Son to be the propitiation for our sins," (I Jn 4:10).

The love with which our Saviour Jesus came with, for our deliverance, was like a flame in His heart and it compelled Him to drink of the cup of suffering with a strong desire. When He knew that the penalty for our sins was very severe, He prepared to bear it, in our stead, "Greater love has no one than this, than to lay down one's life for his friends," (Jn 15:13). We are reminded of the heroic acts of many valiant people such as the father who enters a burning house in order to save his children, the young man who swims against turbulent waves so that he may rescue someone drowning, or the soldier who remains in his position, even if it means a certain death, in order to save his company. This and many other situations show man in his most sublime traits and conduct. The more terrible the death and the more voluntary the act, the more glorious the deed becomes. How much more if the death is slow and torturous, such as the death of the cross? How much more if it is for the sake of enemies, "For when we were still without strength, in due time Christ died for the ungodly," (Rom 5:16).

The sacrifice of Christ attained its most supreme manifestation and so the Bible informs us that His voluntary surrender, for the sake of His enemies was the subject of the admiration of Moses and Elijah when they appeared with the Saviour on the mount of transfiguration (Lu 9:31). Great then is the love that is revealed by the death of Christ.

One drop of His sweat in Gethsemane or of His blood that fell upon the cross was sufficient to save the whole world, for every one of His deeds had infinite worth as it emanated from an infinite God. However, His infinite divine generosity and His endless love caused Him to offer His whole being so that the Apostle called it extreme love in his saying, "But God, who is rich in mercy, because of His great love with which He loved us, even when we were dead in trespasses, made us alive together with Christ," (Eph 2:4-5). When Zacharias spoke of the grace that God determined to bestow upon the world through the death of Christ, he did not say that it arose through His mercy but, through His tender mercy (Lu 1:78).

The meaning of the cross and the meaning of "the death of Christ on our behalf," then is love. The goal of this is that, as the Apostle says, "We love Him because He first loved us," (I Jn 4:19). So did His death affect us and have we understood from it that He loves us? Have we matched this love with our own? How callous we must be that we should not be affected after all that! St John Chrysostom said, "It is not the fire of hell and its eternal suffering that makes us love God, but the sight of Jesus crucified".

What then compelled Jesus to die for the sake of man's salvation? No one forced Him but He is the One who sacrificed Himself for us in obedience to His Father. Had He forsaken the world, it would have degenerated into misery and fallen into eternal damnation as what He has done to the rebellious angels when they oppressed us and He would have lost none of His glory. His excellent love did not permit that we should be driven to everlasting death and His mercy arranged this amazing plan that had perplexed the mind of man. It caused the sentence that had been imposed on fallen man, to be transfered to the Only-Begotten Son. So, the holy and righteous One died instead of the wretched sinner.

It was possible for Him to reveal His love for us in another way. He did not want to send us an angel as He did not will to see another bind our wounds. What a great and indescribable love, the fire of which was not extinguished by the flood of pain that had been poured upon it but it was like a furnace that was ignited by water. The measure of the wounds in the body of Jesus is that of the rising flames of love toward us. As once was contemplated, "The cheers heard for the Saviour as He entered Jerusalem were not as pleasant a happening, to Him, as the callous cries of "Crucify Him! Crucify Him!" for love had transformed the bitterness of the cross into sweetness."

The love of Christ and His compassion were so inflamed that, for our sakes, He allowed His garments to be removed and to be crucified naked. His love caused Him to call His suffering a drink and His death a baptism as He said to the sons of Zebedee, "Are you able to drink the cup that I am about to drink, and be baptized with the baptism that I am baptized with?" (Matt 20:22). It is obvious that one of the properties of water is to cool internally, and externally. So His internal pain was to Him as a drink and His external as a bathing and this is love that cannot be described. As described in the book ok of Songs, "Go forth, O daughters of Zion, And see King Solomon with the crown With which his mother crowned him On the day of his wedding, The day of the gladness of his heart," (Song 3:11). So the day of Christ's death, He considers as the day of His wedding for in it He tendered His bride's dowry.

How great is Your love for us Jesus that has made You desire death in order to save us, so that even when Peter reproached You and said, "Far be it from You, Lord; this shall not happen to you," You rebuked him saying, "Get behind Me, Satan! You are an offense to Me, for you are not mindful of the things of God, but the things of men," ((Matt 16:23). As if to say, "I yearn for this death which burns within Me. Do you, then, wish to take this opportunity away from Me when I have reached it?" For this reason we find that the Bible says of the Lord before He left with His disciples for Gethsemane, "And when they had sung a hymn, they went out to the Mount of Olives," (Matt 26:30). So before His affliction He was singing and what He saw then was not His agony or His cross but the salvation of mankind and His joy at their salvation overcame His sorrow.

What callousness of heart is this that cannot esteem the love of Christ after He had loved us so and had washed away our sins with His blood? Who could refrain from cleaving to Him when they recall that He had spread His hands on the cross accepting, welcoming and eagerly embracing all who take refuge in Him?

One of the fathers said, "Any love not emanating from the suffering of the Saviour or profound contemplation on it and full submission to it, is a vain love."

God loves His Only-Begotten with an infinite love but despite this He surrendered Him to suffer all kinds of terrible tortures. Why this ruthlessness toward the blameless Son? It is nothing other than that He had offered Himself a ransom on our behalf and His compassionate Father was content with this. God's love for us caused Him to be hard with the Son. Let us chant, then, singing, "He who did not spare His own Son, but delivered Him up for us all, how shall He not with Him also freely give us all things?" (Rom 8:32).

What should you do now, my beloved? How deeply should you sigh and bitterly weep if you truly believe that He who was crucified was your God and Creator and had granted you more than a father does his son and a mother her daughter? What should you do if you believe that the reason He had resorted to drinking this bitter suffering was His love for you and His purpose your salvation. For this He was content to come down from heaven and yield Himself up to the cross.

All of nature was disturbed upon seeing the Son of God hanging on the cross for my sake, I fallen man and my heart alone had remained hard unwilling to soften. O cross of Christ, the hope of the weak and counsellor of the ignorant. O Ark of the

New Covenant and the repose of Solomon. O You alone Who gives comfort to the dejected and solace to the faithful. Grant utterance to my feeble lips, tears to my rigid eyes and tenderness to my heart that is not affected by the death of my beloved Redeemer Jesus Christ.

If one of our friends does us a small favour we respond with thanks and gratitude, so why do we harden our hearts toward our true Friend Jesus Who has granted us His life. If an enemy had risked something for us we would meet him with abundant love rather than with enmity and coldness. Can we not at least deal with Jesus in the same manner? Even if He had shed just a single tear for the sake of our salvation we should spend our lives jubilant in feelings of gratitude for Him. As St Ambrose contemplated, "I am indebted to You, my Master Jesus Christ, not because You created me for in the work of creation You only said one word and everything came into being, but my debt to You is great because You have redeemed me. Your redemptive work has caused to bear what the whole world could not bear.

Christian churches have arranged the Feast of the cross in order to place before our eyes Christ crucified, wounded and pierced in His side, to revisit His groans and pain and to declare His favour. Let our eyes be opened so that springs of tears may flow from them to prove our union with Him in His pain and suffering. We hear of what had befallen Him without being moved. The more His heart is filled with compassion for us, the more our souls are bereft of any emotion that draws us to Him.

This should not be so, my beloved, for we not only deny His love but we also become collaborators with His crucifiers and slaughterers. With our lips we feign love for Him but in reality we are enemies. This is because every day, we renew His crucifixion with our sins, and with our offences we repeatedly disdain His blood which was shed for our sakes. His crucifiers were no greater offenders or sinners than we are. There are, amongst us, some who have weighed down His cross with their wickedness, some who have mocked His religion as Herod did and some who have pierced His brow with thorns of transgression and have driven into His body nails of the denial of His favour and grace. Some of us have stabbed Him, not with a single spear but with many spears of our various misdeeds.

What can we say except that God has perfected us with His goodness and we have altogether accepted our wickedness by scorning the suffering of our Saviour? He died to give us life and we live to renew, with our transgressions, His agony and death. In the law of Moses it is written, "If anyone is found slain, lying in the field in the land which the LORD your God is giving you to possess, and it is not known who killed him, then your elders and your judges shall go out and measure the distance from the slain man to the surrounding cities. And it shall be that the elders of the city nearest to the slain man will take a heifer which has not been worked and which has not pulled with a yoke. The elders of that city shall bring the heifer down to a valley with flowing water, which is neither ploughed nor sown, and they shall break the heifer's neck there in the valley. Then the priests, the sons of Levi, shall come near, for the LORD your God has chosen them to minister to Him and to bless in the name of the LORD; by their word every controversy and every assault shall be settled. And all the elders of that city nearest to the slain man shall wash their hands over the heifer whose neck was broken in the valley. Then they shall answer and say, 'Our hands have not shed this blood, nor have our eyes seen it,'" (Deut 21:1-7). Let us then ascend Golgotha and listen to the crucified One as He cries out that among us there are those who have killed Him and those who have crucified, offended and stabbed Him. Can we then wash our hands of the matter and say that we are innocent?

Can one who has a wicked tongue say that he has not pierced His side with his depraved words? Can he who is self-centred claim that he has not killed Him by selfishly hurting others? Can he who robs others pretend that he has not slapped Him with His guilty hands? Can he who chases after immorality say that he has not nailed His hands and feet with his vile deeds?

The man who is known to return evil for good, loses affection in the hearts of all. A Roman senator once wanted to reproach a citizen for killing his mother so he said to him, "You have killed your mother and that is enough to grieve you so what more can I say to you?" It is also enough to say to a sinner, "You are he who has crucified your Lord and you still crucify Him with your sins. What greater evil can you do?"

Our sins are what have caused our Saviour to suffer and be crucified, do we then persist in loving them. Who would have believed, had he not experienced this for himself, that there can exist people with such cruel hearts and violent manners to truly know that sin is the cause of the death of their God on their behalf and yet invite it into their homes and entertain it in their hearts and enjoy committing it after it has become an unjust executioner of Him Who had redeemed them with His blood? Sin is the slaughterer of Christ and despite this they conceal it in their hearts. One of the saints addressed Christ saying, "What has caused You to endure all this brutal anguish - love or madness? Indeed love and madness together, for the love is Yours and the madness is mine. Love made You shed Your blood to save me, and madness is what makes me renew Your cross by committing the most horrendous sins."

Are you not ashamed, you who scorn the love of God? You deserve to at least be thrown into hell's fire. As St Paul says, "Of how much worse punishment, do you suppose, will he be thought worthy who has trampled the Son of God underfoot, counted the blood of the covenant by which he was sanctified a common thing, and insulted the Spirit of grace?" (Heb 10:29). And He also said, "If anyone does not love the Lord Jesus Christ, let him be accursed," (I Cor 16:22). A sinful Christian is thankless of the kindness shown by His Saviour Who loved him and died for him. Moses had addressed the Israelites, even before the incarnation, saying, "Love the LORD your God with all your heart," (Deut 6:5). What then, should Christians do after the fact of the incarnation? It is said that two brothers were on opposite sides of a civil war and it happened that one unknowingly killed the other. When the surviving brother discovered this, he lit a fire beside the body of his brother and said sorrowfully, "My brother, forgive me for I have unwittingly killed you!" He then proceeded to stab himself with a knife and to throw himself onto the flame. What then should a Christian, who intentionally offends Jesus his firstborn Brother do?

Look to the cross of your Redeemer and contemplate your Saviour as He dies, arms outstretched, side ruptured and heartbroken, turning with eyes lowered to each one of us saying, "I am dying for you and if I had to endure death a thousand times I would, out of love for you. You see My blameless body torn by whips and soaked with blood and you see Me struggling and surrendering the spirit and drowning in a sea of agony. The greatest tortures for Me, however, are your sins and enduring suffering for the sake of ungrateful people. I died to save you so why do you wish to destroy yourself?"

Suppose that our hearts were harder than the rocks that were split at the time of the crucifixion, would we be able to withstand these passionate reproaches? If only His anguished tears and the flow of His blood would cut off the flow of our sins and instil in our hearts a burning love so we may say with St Paul, "The love of Christ compels us," (2 Cor 5:14).

Let us altogether say to this perfect God, "You have willed Lord to open Your side to ease our way that we may know the depth of Your love for us and take cover in it. Indeed Lord there is nothing in Your heart but love for us, and if we should forget everything else, we cannot forget the image of Your death, that is the image of Your love."

Why do I see you loving the world and all that is in it? Who should have been the subject of your love? You love your family and your friends none of whom have died for you yet are oblivious as to Whom it was that has saved you from death. As someone once said, "How can I, O Lord my God, after You have entirely proven Your powerful and extravagant love for me, despise and denounce this love?"

When one of the saints considered the sacrifice of the Saviour against the deeds of mankind, he wandered the streets weeping and calling out saying, "Love is not loved." By this he meant that people repay God's love with enmity.

It is said that a man had violently hit Socrates, the Greek philosopher, on his face till it was swollen and bruised but Socrates had not resist. All he did later was to write across his own forehead the words, "So-and-so (naming the man) did this." Likewise Jesus today roams the city to ponder the condition of those for whom

He had suffered and died and finds them indulging in wickedness, not resisting sin and profaning His name at every opportunity, so He weeps and His tears seem to say, "Those, for whom I died, did this.

If Jacob served his uncle numerous years for the love he had for Rachel, how can we not devote our lives to the service of Jesus for the sake of the beauty of His deep love? A man was in the habit of going to a graveyard and planting flowers at a particular grave. When someone asked him why he does that, he replied, "When it came time for me to go to war, I was delayed for important reasons, and so this man went in my stead and faithfully performed all duties that were mine until he died in the war." The gilded inscription on the tomb read, He died for me. If this then is the response to being saved by someone from one's temporal and mortal death, what should be the response to Jesus, Who through His own death, saves us from everlasting death?

How I do not devote my life to serve God, for His great and deep love to me?

At a certain exhibition, there are a series of three paintings depicting the stages in a soul's response to the crucifixion. In the first, a man stands before the crucified Christ meditating and questioning without realising the mystery for which God allowed the blameless to die. The second shows the same man kneeling before the cross having understood the words of Isaiah, "The chastisement for our peace was upon Him, And by His stripes we are healed," (Isa 53:5) and with a thankful heart deeming Jesus to be his Lord and Redeemer. In the last we see him beneath the cross, having dedicated his life to the service of his Saviour.

If then you know that you commit a great a crime by not

loving Him Who loves you, you must regret the life you have wasted away from Him and spend the rest in His love. When David heard of the death of Jonathan his beloved, he tore his clothes (2 Sam 1:11). Now that you have heard of the death of your beloved Jesus, why do I see you unmoved? I , my Saviour, am indeed blind not perceiving this, Your great love, so open my eyes to see You, as You opened the eyes of the thief on Your right. Then will I seek my salvation.

Know that what love requires of us is not what it required of Him. It does not require of us to be crowned with thorns or for our hands to be nailed but that to stab our desires and lusts with the spears of prayer and to nail our pleasures with the words of God. Then we can offer what we can to repay God's love, not with words but with deeds, "My little children, let us not love in word or in tongue, but in deed and in truth," (I Jn 3:18).

Jesus, grant that we may love You with all our hearts, with all our souls and with all our might. There is nothing for us but You, in heaven or on earth. I am crushed whenever I remember that my sin is what has removed You from my heart and separated me from You. You are my portion and my repose. You are my comfort and my life. You are the One who loved me so grant that I may cry out with St Paul saying, "Who shall separate us from the love of Christ?" (Rom 8:35). Because I know that it is sin that distances me from You, help me to overcome it through Your honoured blood. Fill me with Your grace that it may support me whenever I am besieged. If You are with me I will prevail and will overcome it and sever my ties with it. Here is the heart that You have redeemed ready for Your habitation. Here it is prepared as a temple for Your Holy Spirit.

Your heart may have dissolved but not the fire of Your love.

Grant, Lord, that I may acquire even a spark from this flame in Your pure heart, to place in my own that my soul may be filled with Your love. The blaze of my love for You will then burn all my wicked thoughts: the love of money, the love of the world and the pride of life.

My good saviour your heart has melted in you, not from the natural fire but from the burning love you have for me, please God give me a flame from your pure love to burn off all of the evil thoughts in me and wipe out the love of the world and the love of the money.

CHAPTER 15

On Contemplating the Cross

"For I determined not to know anything among you except
Jesus Christ and Him crucified" (1Cor 2:2)

The first thing that amazes the believer as he stands before the
cross is the over abundance of God's love. Whoever probes deeply
into the mysteries of the Saviour's suffering, appreciates that on
the cross, God has accomplished a matter worthy of wonder and
awe. Indeed, my faithful Saviour, the mind is bewildered whenever
it contemplates Your agony. Who can express what He endured
upon the cross? I see You as those nails hold up Your body and
ponder the wounds in Your hands and feet that intensified Your
pain as they enlarged. I consider how all Your organs and senses
were affected by severe pain as if each was bearing its own cross.

How can I not wonder when Your eyes, before which all are
revealed (Heb 4:13), are pained by the sight of blood flowing
from Your wounds? How can I not be amazed at Your ears, which
hear the groans of the afflicted and now are wounded by the
abuse hurled at them? How can I not marvel when the tongue,
that had uttered a word and the world came into being, is now
being scorched by thirst and convulses due to the gall and sour
wine? How can I not be baffled when I see thorns penetrating
Your beautiful head before which angels and men bow? Nails
pierce Your capable hands, which brought heaven and earth into
existence and nails tear Your pure feet that knew no rest while You
were on earth striving for the salvation of the world.

My beloved Jesus, what Christian who is taught by faith that
You died on the cross out of love for him could not love You from
the depth of their heart. Truly Lord, I stoop beneath Your cross
entreating You to forgive my guilt for the time I spent unable to
appreciate Your love for me. I fear death whenever I consider my

sins, yet I am revived and my hope in my salvation is rekindled when I see the pure blood flowing from Your holy wounds. Then I cry out, "There is therefore now no condemnation to those who are in Christ Jesus, who do not walk according to the flesh, but according to the Spirit," (Rom 8:1).

Yes, my Lord, I offer You what is left of my life and commit between Your hands (those that were nailed to the cross) my whole heart with all my desires for You to wash with Your honoured blood, sanctify and yield from it springs of holy yearning.

One of the saints had this meditation, "He who desires to abide in the love of our Lord Jesus Christ must imagine the Saviour hanging on the cross, dead for the sake of his eternal salvation," The soul that loves to contemplate the cross cannot be tempted by Satan to despair of its salvation. This is because the blood of the Son of God becomes for it a perpetual spring of consolation and opens wide for it the door to hope. If Satan parades before it the vain glory of the world and its pleasures, it will be granted a heavenly grace, emanating from the cross, to quench and eradicate any longing for the world and to give it a life of contempt of all that is in the world and a desire for the heavenly glory.

O you who are fixed firmly to the cross, when the hour of death is upon you, Satan will attack you to cut off your hope by parading before you all those sins you committed here on earth. Do not be anxious but turn your gaze to the crucified One and cry out with all confidence and hope saying, "Remember me my Saviour and Redeemer for I am the fruit of Your suffering and death upon the cross."

Jesus Christ said, "And I, if I am lifted up from the earth, will draw all peoples to Myself," (Jn 12:32), meaning that His death upon the cross is what draws hearts to Him. St Paul also says, "But we preach Christ crucified," (I Cor 1:23). For how many people would a single glance at the cross have been sufficient for them to leave all and follow Him, to abandon the world and its vainglory, and sin and its pleasures, and to feel a happiness that can only be fulfilled in Jesus the crucified?

St Augustine contemplated, "Whoever looks to the crucified Jesus and places his trust in Him, will be healed of the wounds of his sin,". Let the image of the crucified Jesus be continually before you and say with the Apostle, "For I determined not to know anything among you except Jesus Christ and Him crucified," (I Cor 2:2).

Meditate upon the sacrifice of the Son of God for it has washed away our sins as the Spirit of truth testifies, "To Him who loved us and washed us from our sins in His own blood," (Rev 1:5). So no matter the weight of our sins, if we look to this holy sacrifice we will find that the noose of the burden of our offences has loosened and fallen from around our necks leaving us in complete repose.

Come forward to the throne of God with a sincere and faithful heart. Is not the way prepared and sanctified through blood? So cross it with courage. Is not the veil of enmity lifted? Enter then without fear or dread. Has not the door been opened to you to the throne of grace? Ascend to it immediately without hesitation or uncertainty but rather with determination, haste and sure confidence. Is not the One who redeemed you the same as He who sits on that throne? Believe in Him then and do not sadden Him with your lack of faith. No matter how sinful you are, He is prepared to accept you wholly, to forgive all your transgressions and to cleanse you from all your sins.

Yes, go to Him you sinner and catch the drops of blood falling from the cross and wash with them your heart to purify it and then you will be worthy to see God (Matt 5:8). The beloved Son will never reject anyone who comes to Him in love. So throw your sins before Him, as the sinful woman did, and He will lift them from you and restore to you your purity, your joy and your bliss.

How can we describe the work of God upon the cross other saying that it is the work of mercy and love? You cannot gaze upon the cross without crying out and saying, "God is love". The God of love is He who calls you and with the love, that made Him surrender His Son for your sake, accepts you willingly and happily.

My beloved Jesus, when You were lifted upon the cross, we became Your possession and were restored to You. Bind us with Your cross by the power of Your love and help us to endure pain and sorrow clinging as a baby to his mother. We wish to lose all, that we may gain You the only precious Stone. Empty us Lord of all but the grace of Your holy love.

CHAPTER 16

The Benefits of Contemplating the Sufferings of Christ

"But God forbid that I should boast except in the cross
of our Lord Jesus Christ" (Gal 6:14)

St Augustine said, "Nothing could be as beneficial as contemplating what Jesus endured for our sakes upon the cross. No remedy could be as effective for the healing of our wounded souls as the continuous contemplation on the suffering of Christ,". Contemplating Christ's suffering helps us to resist temptation and to have a fervent spirit in our service to Him. As one of the saints noted, "He who trains himself through meditation on the life of Christ and His suffering will find in it all he needs and will want nothing else."

Love makes us prolong our reflection on the subject of our love and this delights the loved one. For this reason a mother who has a son who is away, rejoices more when she hears that he always remembers her than for the many gifts he sends her. So it is with Christ Who rejoices more when He knows that we always meditate on His great favour evident in His death on the cross than when we undertake any other duty.

One night when King Xerxes could not sleep he ordered the book of the chronicles of his reign to be brought in and read to him. He found in it the service rendered by Mordecai the Jew who had exposed those conspiring to assassinate the king. What is required of Christians is to keep vigil while acknowledging the great service rendered them by the Lord Jesus Christ by saving them from everlasting death through His own honourable death.

The saints who have preceded us spent their lives contemplating the suffering of Christ and have finally reached the harbour of salvation in peace. Ask those who offered themselves to die, what gave them the courage to do that and they will reply that it was the precious wounds of the Saviour. Ask those who were patient in their tribulation and steadfastly endured torture, what gave them strength and they will reply that it was the long-suffering of Jesus in the midst of suffering. Ask those who have triumphed for the reason of their victory and they will declare that it was by contemplating the cross of Christ. When St John Chrysostom wanted to describe how to delve into and meditate upon the cross of Christ he said, "Contemplating the cross is better than being adorned with myriads of crowns, for the crown adorns the head but contemplating the cross guards the mind and is the banner of victory over Satan, the remedy for the healing of the sicknesses of the soul and the power to triumph over all our adversaries."

Another saint also noted, "Truly, the cross is a mysterious book written in the blood of the Son of God Himself. Through it God and all His attributes, especially the attribute of love, are revealed completely. Moreover, we should call the cross a library, for from it we learn the science of eternal life, read of the mystery of the glorious salvation and comprehend how God loved us and reconciled us to Himself through the blood of His Son," Look to the cross to find relief from the heavy burden of sin. You who are grieving meditate on it and you will attain supreme comfort.

He who thinks upon the cross, knowing that Christ suffered for the sins of the world and remains unmoved is not mindful of it, is no different to those soldiers who divided up His garments then sat down to watch Him unconcerned. Jesus has fulfilled what was required of Him to do on earth; will you do what is required of you? A painting, by Domenico Feti, entitled "Ecce Homo" ("Behold the Man") shows Jesus with a crown of thorns on His head. At the bottom of the painting, the artist painted the words: This I have done for you. What have you done for Me?

Contemplating on the cross produces very good fruits. St Paul asks us to recollect the suffering of Christ and to reflect upon it saying, "For as often as you eat this bread and drink this cup, you proclaim the Lord's death till He comes," (I Cor 11:26).

Some of the fruits of contemplating the cross:

I. Remorse over sin

Nothing reveals to us the aggravation caused by the wickedness of sin like Christ's suffering. As was contemplated by one of the saints, "Know that not the eternal punishment reserved for sinners or anything else can alert us to the weight of sin like meditating on the fact that God became that He may redeem us."

Christ suffered because of sin and He is the One who reveals to us its ugliness. In the words of another, "If God throws all people in hells fire, it wouldn't even satisfy His justice, yet Christ's incarnation and death is more than sufficient." Therefore, our reflection on the cross powerfully leads us to regret and sorrow over our sins.

The Bible says, "They shall look on Him whom they pierced," (Jn 19:37). Indeed we have pierced Him with the spears of our sins, so what is left for us to do but to pierce our own hearts with the spears of contrition and brokenness and to scrape out the filth with the blade of confession.

A saint reflected, "I used to play and take leisurely walks in the streets while I was being sentenced to death by the King's assembly and I was oblivious. The King's only Son heard of this and He removed the crown from His head and the royal robe and went out secretly, wearing a contemptible garment. When I saw Him in this painful state I was astonished and bewildered and I asked Him for the reason. He answered that He was on His way to die in my stead. What should have been done at this time?

Any man would have been totally insensitive and monstrous had he not abandoned his play and everything else to accompany the Son of the King weeping with Him."

O cruel heart, cry out to Your Master saying, "How can I love sin my Saviour when it is what has thrown You into the greatest suffering and severest pain? I am he who deserved that cross and these insults that You endured for my sake Jesus. I detest and despise you, O sin, because You caused my Saviour Jesus to be hung on the wood of the cross."

Our contemplation on the suffering of Christ makes us grieve over our sin so God can forgive us and preserve us from it. Our regret will also help us not to revert to it.

2. Recognition of God's favour and thankfulness for it

Who can contemplate the death of Christ and refrain from giving thanks for His favour and goodness. The Saviour said to His disciples after washing their feet, "Do you know what I have done to you?" (Jn 13:12) and today He says to everyone who has denied His favour, "Do you know what I have done to you? If you would know, O ungrateful one, what I have done to you, you would devote your life to endlessly giving thanks. If you would raise your sights to the cross and know that I, while am the Word, took flesh and died for your sake, you would not hesitate to give Me your whole heart and to be engrossed in My love."

St John Chrysostom had this to say, "One of the attributes of the good servant is to consider His master's common favours as intended for him alone, and that he alone is indebted for it and bound to repay the kindness," and St Paul concurs, "who loved me and gave Himself for me," (Gal 2:20). So should each one of us say, since we all benefit from the death of Christ as if Christ had died for each alone. Just as the rays of the sun shine on me as if it shines on no one else, so the incarnation, crucifixion and death of the Son of God profit me as if they had transpired for me alone.

Our Saviour wants us to increase in our knowledge of His grace not because He is in need of our recognition but to make us worthy of new favours. As one of the saints says, "Doubt in and forgetfulness of the grace we have received from God is akin to a wind that dries out the spring of divine mercy and obstructs the stream of heavenly blessings."

The Saviour said to the demon-possessed man who was healed by Him, "Return to your own house, and tell what great things God has done for you," (Lk 8:39). Had this man not spoken and declared his Master's act of kindness, we would have considered him ungrateful and a denier of good. Unfortunately we are guilty of this very same fault and we do not reproach ourselves. Do we feel that we discern the goodness of our Saviour, thank Him continuously and always proclaim His blessings? No, we do not thank Him that He has redeemed us but rather we grumble against Him because He has not given us abundant riches. We do not care that He toiled for our salvation from eternal destruction but our care is limited to the attainment of worldly glory. If we sit to sing praises, they are not of His favour but rather of the pleasures of the world and its glory. We are then announcing the esteem of the world not the favours of Jesus.

As one pious man reflected, "O my God Jesus, how did You bear to be crucified for people as hypocritical and as unthankful as we are? Forgive me for daring to speak like this, since zeal for Your glory has compelled me to speak these words. What do

You hope for from mankind? Is it not that they should thank You for Your goodness? Here You see them preferring one of their passions over You, or some paltry profit from the rubble of the world, or a little from the hollow and vain honours of the world. They had sold You in earlier times for thirty pieces of silver, but now sell You for a much smaller price. They swear by Your name falsely, for the sake of a little profit."

3. Strengthening of hope

Contemplating the suffering of Christ, resurrects and refreshes our faith, strengthens our hope and causes us to wholly depend on Him. Everyone who desires to save himself will find, in the death of the Son of God, encouragement for this and will discover that God Himself desires the salvation of man.

St Paul says to us, "For if when we were enemies we were reconciled to God through the death of His Son, much more, having been reconciled, we shall be saved by His life," (Rom 5:10). If God, then, looked on us with the eyes of mercy, when we were enemies in words, deeds and thoughts, how can He not desire our salvation after He has reconciled us to Himself through the blood of His Son?

How can He, who loved us while we were still defiled by sin, not love us now after He had cleansed us with His blood? If He was searching for us while we ran from Him, how can He neglect us now that He has admitted us to His house? This is a firm hope affirmed by the Father, "He who did not spare His own Son, but delivered Him up for us all, how shall He not with Him also freely give us all things," (Rom 8:32).

Do not be afraid to approaching God because of your many

sins, for if He was as harsh as you imagine and if He was to reject accepting you because of your wickedness, He would not have kept you in the world till now but you would have descended to Hades long ago. In His mercy you will be accepted if you will return to Him as said, "Do I have any pleasure at all that the wicked should die?" says the Lord GOD, "and not that he should turn from his ways and live," (Ez 18:23). Depend then on the cross of Christ, approach Him and lean your head against His kind bosom and say, "I come to You now, You who have redeemed me with the blood of Your Son, trusting in Your mercy whenever I see the cross of Your Son. Accept me fully now my Master." Then you will hear the words, "the one who comes to Me I will by no means cast out," (Jn 6:37).

4. The Imitation of Christ

St Augustine said, "The cross was a pulpit in which Christ preached His love." How many are they who follow Jesus, greedy for His kingdom and how few are there who are willing to carry the cross? How many are they who love solace and how few are they who are patient in tribulation. Many follow Jesus in time of peace and few are they who follow Him in time of adversity ... to Golgotha.

The glory of Jesus appeared after the carrying of the cross and we have been promised glory also if we carry the cross. Follow Jesus bearing your suffering, for if you die with Him you will also live with Him. There is no way to heaven except the way of the cross and you cannot exempt yourself from it, you who desires to reach heaven. If you carry the cross willingly, He will carry you and take you to your desired goal. How great is the glory reserved for those who bear suffering with patience for the sake of the name of Jesus? Heaven was separated from earth but the cross united them. All who want to ascend to heaven can only do so through the cross. As someone contemplated, "A single tear shed by you before the cross is sweeter and more desirable to the heart than all the pleasures of the world."

So come and follow your Saviour and strive behind Him carrying the cross and hear Him call to you, "I am the way, the truth, and the life. No one comes to the Father except through Me," (Jn 14:6). Jesus alone is the trusted way to the Kingdom of Heaven.

Thomas a Kempis composed the following dialogue between the faithful and the Saviour in his book The Imitation of Christ:

"The Faithful: O Lord Jesus, forasmuch as Your life was straitened and despised by the world, grant unto me to imitate You in despising the world, for the servant is not greater than his lord, nor the disciple above his master.(Jn 13:16) Let Your servant be exercised in Your life, because there is my salvation and true holiness. Whatsoever I read or hear besides it, it refreshes me not, nor give me delight.

The Saviour: "My son, because you know these things and have read them all, blessed shalt you be if you do them. He who has My commandments and keeps them, he it is that loves Me, and I will love him, and will manifest Myself to him,(John 14:21) and I will make him to sit down with Me in My Father's Kingdom,"

The Faithful: O Lord Jesus, as You have said and promised, even so let it be unto me, and grant me to prove worthy. I have received the cross at Your hand; I have carried it, and will carry it even unto death, as You have laid it upon me. Truly the life of a truly devoted servant is a cross, but it leads to paradise. I have begun; I may not return back nor leave it.

Come, my brothers, let us together go forward. Jesus shall be with us. For Jesus' sake have we taken up this cross, for Jesus' sake let us persevere in the cross. He will be our helper, who was our Captain and Forerunner. Behold our King enters in before us, and He will fight for us. Let us follow bravely, let no man fear terrors; let us be prepared to die bravely in battle, and let us not so stain our honour, as to fly from the cross."

5. The most important lesson of humility

Meditate upon Him for while being an incarnate God, He humbled Himself even to the extent of bearing the most atrocious abuse. Take a lesson that will enable you to reject pride and will prepare you to accept any abuse from people. In order to teach us how to walk the way of humility He, in His dignity, walked in it Himself. And in order to show us as contemptible as we are, the merit of being characterized by humility He, as great and majestic as He is, was distinguished by it. If a commander wishes to encourage his soldiers in combat, he takes a sword in his own hands and leads them in combat as one of them. Similarly, when the Saviour wanted to attract us to humility and to make us reject pride, He placed Himself at the lowest level and said to His disciples, "For who is greater, he who sits at the table, or he who serves? Is it not he who sits at the table? Yet I am among you as the One who serves," (Lk 22:27), and "whoever desires to become great among you, let him be your servant. And whoever desires to be first among you, let him be your slave — just as the Son of Man did not come to be served, but to serve, and to give His life a ransom for many," (Matt 20:26-28). St. Augustine tell us that "Humility is the foundation of all the virtues; therefore, in a soul where it does not exist there can be no true virtue, but the mere appearance only. In like manner, it is the most proper disposition for all celestial gifts. And, finally, it is so necessary to perfection, that of all the ways to reach it, the first is humility; the second, humility; the third, humility. And if the question were repeated a hundred times, I should always give the same answer."

6. Forbearance in suffering

Christ traversed hardships before us and accepted them with patience and bore them with thanksgiving so that we do not become wearied by them. St Paul said, "For consider Him who endured such hostility from sinners against Himself, lest you become weary and discouraged in your souls," (Heb 12:3) and St Peter said, "For what credit is it if, when you are beaten for your faults, you take it patiently? But when you do good and suffer, if you take it patiently, this is commendable before God. For to this you were called, because Christ also suffered for us, leaving us an example, that you should follow His steps: 'Who committed no sin, Nor was deceit found in His mouth'; who, when He was reviled, did not revile in return; when He suffered, He did not threaten, but committed Himself to Him who judges righteously," (I Pet 2:20-23).

Since we now know the greatness of the benefits of contemplating the cross, let us prolong our gaze at it receiving divine commandments and walking in them saying, "O glorious cross of the Saviour, to you we lift our eyes as a handmaiden lifts her eyes toward her mistress. Open our eyes that we may see wonders from Your cross. May Your Spirit be with us when we look to the cross to make known to us what is needed. Strengthen us Lord with Your grace that we may live looking to the cross, so that when the time of departure comes we will be looking at and trusting in it."

CHAPTER 17

On The Necessity of Our Death With Christ and Living For Him

"Now if we died with Christ, we believe that we shall also live with Him"
(Rom 6:8)

In Adam all die (I Cor 15:22) and Adam is a type of Christ (Rom 5:14). No doubt that all partake in the death of Christ for, "we were buried with him through baptism into death," (Rom 6:4) and have become after that separated from sin, as the dead is separated from the living. The union of the believer to Christ through baptism is like dying, with Him, to sin. There is no longer the slightest relationship between the believer and sin with regards to the practise, the authority or the pleasure. We are separated from the world considering Jesus to be our portion, as Christ was separated from the visible world while in the tomb.

It is not enough for us to value the suffering of our Saviour or to be moved by it, for we can be moved without knowing anything about the efficacy and power of His blood. The death of Christ is a monumental reality but we benefit nothing from it if our faith does not take us into a personal fellowship with Him and with His suffering. The meaning of Christ dying for me is that when He died, I died also. Now it seems that, in the sight of God, the sentence of death for my sins has been imposed on me and I am deemed to have died as far as sin is concerned.

How do we die to sin? By abandoning it. By not attaching ourselves to it. By not thinking upon it, looking at it, hearing it or talking about it. By self-denial and by surrendering ourselves fully to Christ. By total submission to Him, for if we surrender all but one of our senses to Christ we are not dead to sin. And if we close all doors except one, we are not dead to sin.

In Greek mythology, Achilles was the son of the Thessalian King Peleus and the nymph Thetis. According to legend, Thetis wished to make Achilles immortal, by dipping him in the subterranean River Styx and she succeeded with the exception of the heel by which she held him. During the Trojan War he was killed by a poisoned arrow which struck the vulnerable spot in his heel. This story alerts us to the need for complete burial with Christ. There must not remain any small element within us that is not in submission to Him. When Satan sees a person accepting Christ as his Saviour, he will do his utmost to lay his hands on even the smallest part of him. He desires to have even the slightest authority over us to ensure our fall, for he knows that if he prevents our complete burial with Christ, he will prevent our complete death to sin.

The true believer deems himself dead before all the demands of sin. Sin has no power over the dead, for even if sin were to adorn itself in the most captivating and seductive form, it would still be unable to move that dead person. Tears, smiles and sweet melodies would not receive a reaction from that cold corpse which will never respond untill it hears the voice of the Son of God. This is our position with regards to sin. God looks at us as if we have been crucified with Christ and have died with Him as the Apostle declared, "And those who are Christ's have crucified the flesh with its passions and desires. ... by whom the world has been crucified to me, and I to the world," (Gal 5:24, 6:14). The world has been crucified to the believer that is he was previously attached to it but when he believed in the crucified Christ, the world became crucified and dead to him and had no power over him or any attraction in his eyes. So the beautiful young woman, who had captivated hearts with her beauty loses this attraction after her death, and in fact becomes repugnant as her beauty is transformed to hideousness. A faithful person, before believing, looked on the world as beautiful but after gaining his faith he sees it as a corpse that has been marred by corruption.

The believer is also crucified to the world. He who is crucified and has died loses all sensation so no matter how beautiful the world is in the eyes of the living, it does not appear that way as seen by the dead. The world and all its lusts is invisible to the believer and he does not feel its existence, for he has died to it and the dead does not feel anything around him as St Paul demonstrates also, "knowing this, that our old man was crucified with Him, that the body of sin might be done away with, that we should no longer be slaves of sin. For he who has died has been freed from sin. ... Therefore do not let sin reign in your mortal body, that you should obey it in its lusts. And do not present your members as instruments of unrighteousness to sin, but present yourselves to God as being alive from the dead, and your members as instruments of righteousness to God," (Rom 6:6-7,12-13).

The believer does not only die to sin but also lives to righteousness, for Christ Who died for our sins, rose for our justification (Rom 4:25). I the sinner who was crucified on Golgotha, when I throw myself onto this cross and consider myself dead, then I will enter the life of the risen Christ and will become in Him alive for righteousness, and in Him I will be strengthened to continue in the new life, "we were reconciled to God through the death of His Son, much more, having been reconciled, we shall be saved by His life," (Rom 5:10). "Just as Christ was raised from the dead by the glory of the Father, even so we also should walk in newness of life, (Rom 6:4). Just as Christ rose and lives a new life other than the one before, so too we must rise spiritually and live a new life different to the old one where we were enslaved by the passions of the body.

The Apostle asserts, "I have been crucified with Christ; it is no longer I who live, but Christ lives in me; and the life which I now live in the flesh I live by faith in the Son of God, who loved me and gave Himself for me," (Gal 2:20). My death with Christ in one aspect does not preclude life in another, for that to which I die is different to that for which I live. Death is to sin and life is for righteousness, "Likewise you also, reckon yourselves to be dead indeed to sin, but alive to God in Christ Jesus our Lord," (Rom 6:11). "Who Himself bore our sins in His own body on the tree, that we, having died to sins, might live for righteousness," (1 Pet 2:24).

Death was not able to hold Christ and is not able to hold us if we are in Christ. What then is after death and burial? Resurrection, "I am He who lives, and was dead," (Rev 1:18). When we are buried with Christ, not only will our sins be forgiven, but the power of God will come upon us, "according to the working of His mighty power which He worked in Christ when He raised Him from the dead," (Eph 1:19-20) and with this power we can do all things through Christ who strengthens us (Phil 4:13). We can reject the world and walk in the newness of life. Someone once said, "I desire to die that I may live. I desire to die to all temporal earthly affections in order to live for the eternal love of Jesus Christ."

It is not fitting then that a person should call himself a faithful Christian and then live in sin, "for he who has suffered in the flesh has ceased from sin," (1 Pet 4:1). That is he who has died to sin through Christ's death must live a life of holiness as proven by the words of St Paul, "How shall we who died to sin live any longer in it," (Rom 6:2) and "Therefore, if you died with Christ from the basic principles of the world, why, as though living in the world,....." (Col 2:20).

He who desires to live the life of faith must hear the words of the Apostle, "that you put off, concerning your former conduct, the old man which grows corrupt according to the deceitful lusts, and be renewed in the spirit of your mind, and that you put on the new man which was created according to God, in true righteousness and holiness," (Eph 4:22-24). The citizens of this world perceive that the new man is completely different to the old in thoughts, words and deeds, as if he were another person. You, O believer, must behave in your life as one who had been bought by the blood of Christ, "because we judge thus: that if One died for all, then all died; and He died for all, that those who live should live no longer for themselves, but for Him who died for them and rose again," (2 Cor 5:14-15).

The believer should live his life for Christ, "For if we live, we live to the Lord; and if we die, we die to the Lord. Therefore, whether we live or die, we are the Lord's. For to this end Christ died and rose and lived again, that He might be Lord of both the dead and the living," (Rom 14:8-9), and, "you are not your own? For you were bought at a price; therefore glorify God in your body and in your spirit, which are God's," (1 Cor 6:19-20).

The death of Christ on the cross gave Him the right to possess every Christian. This is why it is not fitting nor faithful to deny Him full sovereignty over us. He has the right to possess us, for the purchase grants the right and deliverance grants possession. Since Christ purchased us we must surrender ourselves to Him. A sinner was once visiting a village and entered a small church. There he found a painting of Christ's suffering upon the cross and contemplated it for a while. While his eyes were fixed on the sight of tormented love, he noticed these words inscribed under the painting, "Christ lived and died for you. Now, for whom do you live and die?", and His heart melted within him and he immediately surrendered himself to Jesus. He rose up a new man and his whole life changed.

For whom do you wish to live after all that, for your Redeemer or for Satan? For the will of your Heavenly Father or for your own desires? For Him Who died for you or for him who desires your death? Jesus in His love desires that we live for Him for He lived for us and expended His life in His love for us. His love also compels us to offer ourselves to Him as St Paul says, "For the love of Christ compels us," (2 Cor 5:14), that is it obliges us to live for Him.

You Christian ask yourself: "For whom was the life of Christ? Was it not for me? Why then is my life not dedicated completely to Him?"

The life of Christ is for us, for He sacrificed it for us, "who died for us, that whether we wake or sleep, we should live together with Him," (1 Thes 5:10).

And His time is for us, for from the beginning He was planning our salvation, "just as He chose us in Him before the foundation of the world, that we should be holy and without blame before Him in love," (Eph 1:4) and He is at the right hand of the Father making intercession for us now (Rom 8:34) and forever, "we shall always be with the Lord," (1 Thes 4:17).

And His hands are for us, for they were pierced for the salvation of the world, raised in blessing on the day of His Ascension and opened to satisfy all living with His goodness (Ps 104:28).

And His feet are for us, for nails were hammered into them, though He used them in the pursuit of the salvation of the world. Beneath them is our place of rest for how many of the suffering, the sick and the afflicted were, "laid ... down at Jesus' feet, and

He healed them," (Matt 15:30).

And His eyes are for us for they wept for us, "Jesus wept," (Jn 11:35). "The eyes of the LORD are on the righteous," (Ps 34:15). He does not turn His sight from us but always gazes at us with exceptional love. The mother turns her sight from her child but the eyes of the Lord are eternally on us, observing us both day and night, "He who keeps you will not slumber," (Ps 121:3).

And His ears are for us. How many times have they heard the sighs of the downhearted? How many times have they inclined to those in distress? How often have they heard the prayers of the troubled? "His ears are open to their cry ... The righteous cry out, and the LORD hears," (Ps 34:15, 17).

And His voice is for us, for with His tender voice He calls us to open for Him the doors to our hearts, "It is the voice of my beloved! He knocks, saying, 'Open for me, my sister, my love, My dove, my perfect one,'" (Song 5:2) and with it He calls us to His rest, "Come to Me, all you who labour and are heavy laden, and I will give you rest," (Matt 11:28).

And His riches are for us. Is He not the One of whom it is said, "for your sakes He became poor, that you through His poverty might become rich," (2 Cor 8:9).

And His wisdom and knowledge are for us, as St Paul said, "in whom are hidden all the treasures of wisdom and knowledge," (Col 2:3). He uses His wisdom in our refinement and His knowledge in our guidance.

And His heart is for us as He declared when He addressed His Church, "You have ravished my heart, My sister, my spouse," (Song 4:9). How can it be not so when it was He who said, "My heart is like wax; It has melted within Me," (Ps 22:14).

And His love is for us. For if God is love it is because He loves us, "I have loved you with an everlasting love," (Jer 31:3).

What glory do you possess and what happiness have you acquired when your God addresses you saying, "I too am for you!" How do you wish to respond to this faithful speaker?

Answer Him without hesitation, I too am for You!" As He said, "And for their sakes I sanctify Myself, that they also may be sanctified by the truth," (Jn 17:19).

My life is for You Lord, for can I live for another after all You have done for me. For Him I will keep my life. Keep it for Him a life that wanders no longer in the circles of anxiety and confusion, for it has found its true focus and turned toward a sublime goal. You O world! You O Satan! You O sin! There will no longer be any part for you in my life. I have surrendered it to Jesus alone for He alone and no one else died for me.

And my time is for You. I grieve that I do not have a long life in which to serve Him. What is my short life worth if I spend it all in obedience to my Lord? If only I had a thousand lives to dedicate to Him. He guards me day and night and I think about Him day and night. Let me not spend a single minute in the service of another beside Jesus. Who else deserves my time? He has redeemed all my time so let me use it as a holy gift for Christ.

Also my hands are for You. To Him I lift them and if He asks me about what is in them, I will reply that it is the fragrance of the Lord's joy. Indeed Lord, I will shake all worldly dust off my hand so You will say, "This hand is for Me". Indeed, I will not take in it anything evil but will take up with it Your book and will extend it in doing good.

My feet also are for You, for with them I will pursue the way of reconciliation and peace, that I may be worthy of the words, "How beautiful are the feet of those who preach the gospel of peace," (Rom 10:15). I will hasten with them to Your house and ascend Mount Zion and proceed with holy zeal, "I was glad when they said to me, 'Let us go into the house of the LORD'" (Ps 122:1). I will then hear the voice, "do not walk in the way with them," (Prov 1:15), so that my footsteps resemble those of my beloved Master, "who went about doing good," (Acts 10:38).

My voice and my lips are for You, for to You only I will sing and will not move my tongue except in thanks to You and utterance of Your goodness, "It is good to give thanks to the LORD, And to sing praises to Your name, O Most High; To declare Your loving-kindness in the morning, And Your faithfulness every night," (Ps 92:1-2). "My lips shall greatly rejoice when I sing to You, And my soul, which You have redeemed. My tongue also shall talk of Your righteousness all the day long," (Ps 71:23-24). Take my lips O Lord and speak through them. Touch them with a live coal from Your Holy Altar and say to me, "Behold, this has touched your lips; Your iniquity is taken away, And your sin purged," (Is 6:7).

Also all I possess is for You. O Lord I feel that I have nothing to hide from You. Take all I have for I am Yours. Whenever I see the blood pouring from Your side, I scorn all that the world regards as precious, "But what things were gain to me, these I have counted loss for Christ," (Phil 3:7).

My mind and my thoughts are Yours, for it is Your gift to me and should be restored to the Giver. Can I think about anyone but You? I bring every thought into captivity to the obedience of Christ (2 Cor 10:5). The world longs for me to think about it but it is my enemy. You however, are my only Love and it is the most pleasant thing to think about the one you love, "I sat down in his shade with great delight," (Song 2:3). Thinking about You is my happiness, my delight and the joy of my heart, "Search me, O God, and know my heart," (Ps 139:23) so that You may say to me, "The thoughts of the righteous are right," (Prov 12:5).

My will is Yours, for it is You who works in us both to will and to do for Your good pleasure (Phil 2:13). To You I submit my will and even annul it but Your will alone endures, "Your will be done," (Matt 6:10). "not as I will, but as You will," (Matt 26:39). This is because I believe that You love me and that if I surrender my will to You, You will do for my good more than I would for my own.

My heart is for You, "it is good that the heart be established by grace," (Heb 13:9). You said to me "give Me your heart". Take it for it is Yours. Can I bear to allow another to inhabit Your private chambers? It is Your holy throne. Sit upon it and have dominion over it. Create in me a clean heart, a heart that is established in You O Christ that desires no one but You and remains formed in You and then You can enlighten it and make it into a sanctified heaven within me.

My eyes are for You. You look at me so how can I not look at You. "Turn away my eyes from looking at worthless things," (Ps 119:37). Keep them for You that I may lift them to You, (Ps 123:1). Make me see with them the way to heaven, "Open my eyes, that I may see Wondrous things from Your law," (Ps 119:18), that everything but Your face may appear dreadful before me and so that I may look at nothing but You, my dear Saviour.

My ears are for You, for with them I lean to You to hear

Your voice, "My sheep hear My voice, and I know them, and they follow Me," (Jn 10:27). How sweet Your voice is to my ears and how beautiful it is when it falls on them. The sounds of the world smite them for they draw me to destruction but Your voice is sweet for it calls me to eternal glory. Listen then, my ears, incline your hearing to Him and know His voice so that if He calls me I may say to Him, "Speak, LORD, for Your servant hears," (I Sam 3:9).

My love is for You. Here I am listening to Your sweet melodic voice asking me, "Do you love Me?" "Lord, You know all things; You know that I love You," (Jn 21:17). How can I not love You Lord when You created me to love You? I have a store of love that the more I pour out the more it fills up. I cannot love but You for no one thought about me salvation like You. If I love You it is because I am indebted to Your love.

Do you like to look at wickedness? Look but not with the eyes that Christ wept for in order that they may always look to Him.

Do you wish to curse another? Do it but not with the tongue Christ paid a price for on the cross when He drank the gall and sour wine, that we may praise and glorify Him.

Do you wish to walk after evil? Walk but not with the feet, Christ's feet were hammered for that they may walk in His way.

Do you wish to hear vulgar words? Hear but not with the ears for which Christ endured taunts for, that He may preserve them to hear His holy words.

Do you wish to make your heart a place for sin? Do it but not with the heart Christ was stabbed for that it may be a holy temple for His Spirit.

My Lord Jesus, I wish to die for Your love as You did for mine. From now on, I do not wish to live for myself but for You alone. For You I will live and for You I will die, as You lived and died for me, "Draw me away! We will run after you," (Song 1:4).

Let every longing for the world be quenched and may my heart be inflamed with the fire of Your love forever.

CHAPTER 18

The Triumph of the Crucified One

The tragedy of the cross, the equal of which the world had never witnessed, occurred and left a mark against humanity indicating its weakness, cruelty and denial of favour. It left behind dreadful memories to portray for us the extent of the corruption the burden of which all humanity, without exception whether Jewish or Gentile, learned or ignorant, leader or subordinate, had collapsed under. Against the Holy One and the Just they conspired. They renounced Him, the Prince of life, witnessed against Him falsely and killed Him (Acts 3:11-15). Despite the protestation of nature itself and its marvellous proofs, they persisted in their obstinacy and increased it by the Saviour's suffering. How great was their gloating when they heard Him giving up His spirit, (Jn 19:30).

Without doubt the Master died. Mary His mother and the other Mary's were standing near the cross and the tomb and ascertained that He had died, (Jn 19:25).

His enemies left rejoicing and His disciples fled in fear and alarm but affection for Him was hidden in the hearts of friends and loved ones. Joseph of Arimathea asked Pilate if he could take the body of Jesus and Pilate gave him permission. Nicodemus had prepared the finest spices and after they had shrouded Him, they buried Him with reverence in a new carved tomb in a garden (Jn 19:41).

Mary Magdalene, however, could not wait and went early while it was still dark and headed for the place where the Lord was. She was the first to bear the good news of the resurrection to all the disciples and to the entire world and the first to move the breeze of hope to the yearning hearts. How noble and splendid an hour, an hour most delightful and pleasant in which budded a Branch from the house of David, not in the wilderness as when He was crucified but in a garden. He prospered and blossomed, and in the midst of the flowers of Spring He reigned, was exalted and became, "Like an apple tree among the trees of the woods," (Song 2:3). "Go forth, O daughters of Zion, and see King Solomon with the crown," (Song 3:11). The turmoil of the war did not injure Him and as He was, while elevated above all in the realm of Golgotha, resolving with exceptional skill the development of battles, so too after the victory, He precedes us into the garden of peace and prepares a place for us. So be soothed you anxious souls, for your Master is risen and in His resurrection we see:

I. The certainty of the resurrection of the dead, one of the strongest fundamentals of Christianity without which the faith would have no real worth, "But if there is no resurrection of the dead, then Christ is not risen. And if Christ is not risen, then our preaching is empty and your faith is also empty," (I Cor 15:13-14). It is the form of triumph, the majesty of victory, the fruit of exertion, the confirmation of the covenant, the motto of love, the spring of goodness and the epistle of the forthcoming glory. It is the hope of the departed and consolation of those grieving over separation with loved ones. No spiritual pursuit could be accomplished without it and there is no alleviation of the terror of death without its remembrance. With hope we live and with hope we pass away (I Cor 15:30-31).

Always remember, O my soul, the resurrection of your Master to realise the certainty of your own resurrection.

2. Encouragement of the faithful to do good, for if they persevere, certain of eternal life, their sacrifices will become bearable. They will regard the time of their affliction as their

recommendation and therefore will grow in their goodness, "be steadfast, immovable, always abounding in the work of the Lord," (I Cor 15:58), having before their eyes the lofty goal of the crown of glory reserved for the saved righteous.

There is no doubt that the glory of our resurrection and its splendour comes forth from the outburst of our Redeemer's resurrection and the brilliance of its light, "Blessed be the God and Father of our Lord Jesus Christ, who according to His abundant mercy has begotten us again to a living hope through the resurrection of Jesus Christ from the dead, to an inheritance incorruptible and undefiled and that does not fade away, reserved in heaven for you," (I Pet 1:3-4).

In conclusion, we can say that the blessings of the Resurrection are many and cannot be expressed in words. Without it we would have been the most pitiable of all men (I Cor 15:19). It is sufficient that it has abolished the authority of death and sin so that now we can chant with the victorious, "O Death, where is your sting? O Hades, where is your victory?" (I Cor 15:45-55)

CPSIA information can be obtained
at www.ICGtesting.com
Printed in the USA
BVHW03s1428130418
513207BV00002B/149/P

In the wilderness, when Moses the prophet observed the thorn bush unharmed by the flames of fire, he said, "I will now turn aside and see this great sight, why the bush does not burn" (Ex 3:3) and God called to him out of the midst of the bush, and said, "Do not draw near this place. Take your sandals off your feet, for the place where you stand is holy ground." (Ex 3: 5)

As you draw near this awesome sight of The Crucified Jesus, stand in reverence and sever all your worldly attachments. Prepare for the outpouring of grace that will come upon you from the Cross.

Gaze toward the Cross as toward the spring of your salvation, the source of your deliverance, the root of your happiness in this present life and the assurance of attainment of eternal glory in the coming age.

The Crucified Jesus is a 20th century classic that has finally been made available in the English language. It is a group of contemplations on the events that took place during Holy Week, with a special chapter of contemplations on the word of Jesus on the Cross.

ISBN 978-0-9805171-8-7
9000C

ST. SHENOUDA
MONASTERY

9 780980 517187